Momma, You Are Loved

A FORTY-DAY JOURNEY IN GOD'S LOVE

Kimberly Sexton

ISBN 978-1-0980-7802-7 (paperback)
ISBN 978-1-0980-7803-4 (digital)

Christian Faith Publishing, Inc.
832 Park Avenue
Meadville, PA 16335
www.christianfaithpublishing.com

Printed in the United States of America

For my daughter, Emma, and my son, Asher.
May you both always be wrapped up in God's love.
Also, for each and every momma who reads this devotional.
May you always know how truly loved you are.

This is my story, this is my song,
praising my Savior all the day long.

—"Blessed Assurance," Fanny Crosby

FOREWORD

"Give us each day our daily bread" (Luke 11:3 NIV). We all need strength daily to navigate through the very specific challenges we face. Kimberly Sexton has done a phenomenal job with *Momma, You Are Loved.* This devotional is written to help mothers deal with the daily challenges of raising children. Kimberly knows the demands of motherhood to an even greater extent as she raises her beautiful daughter who was diagnosed with type 1 diabetes.

Her honesty and courage are inspirational. This devotional will encourage you and will also help you realize some days are more difficult than others, but God has a way of pulling you through the tough days too. As you add this to your daily spiritual diet, it will give you strength and perspective to thrive no matter what the days may bring.

—Damon Davis
Pastor, New Life Tabernacle

PREFACE

Ever since the birth of my firstborn, Emma, I have come to taste a love from God that I had never known before. This newfound love I experienced opened my eyes to how God truly does feel about me. I had been brought up in church and taught of God by my mother, for whom I am forever grateful, but now I had a connection with Him on a deeper level. I wanted more—so much more that I made the effort to seek Him first every morning, thirsting to be a godly role model for my daughter. Along the way, I realized that His love was not meant for me to hoard up and keep to myself. I became filled with a new desire to share this love with all mommas and help them know how truly loved they are. You are loved by the Highest King and worthy of raising His children whom He gave us as inheritance (Ps. 127:3).

Two years ago, I started writing devotions that sparked from my taste in God's love, which consisted of the everyday moments I experienced with my daughter. While I was writing, I prayed for another child, and God rewarded my womb, allowing me to become pregnant with my son, Asher. I was filled to the brim with love and overflowing with His goodness! Then the unimaginable happened while Asher was still growing in my womb. My firstborn, the daughter who helped me taste God's love, became diagnosed with type 1 diabetes two weeks after her third birthday. An autoimmune disease I knew nothing about had changed our whole world in one single day. Now, a new trial tested my faith in God's love and everything I had been writing about.

Soon, my writings of everyday momma moments became a journey where I desperately needed to stay wrapped up in God's love, a deeper calling into His grace by finding Him in the suffering. A new question arose from the pain, "Do I really know God's love?" I felt as if I could hear God speaking into my heart, *"You had a taste of my love, but you don't truly understand how great My love is"*—a love that I had to learn to take root in, discovering one day at a time by ridding myself of my fleshly nature and filling myself up with His word.

Momma, I invite you to take this forty-day journey with me through real-life momma moments where God's love carried me through. May you allow me into your day and help you feel God wrapping you up into His strong arms. I pray my writings and testimonies will speak life to your heart and open your soul to become rooted in His love.

ACKNOWLEDGEMENTS

This book could not have been possible without the help and support of so many others; therefore, I wish to give honor where honor is due and acknowledge those who have encouraged, motivated, and inspired me to write.

Lord, my rock and my strength, your goodness is too numerous to list one by one. I humbly thank you for laying a new desire in my heart and guiding me in wisdom and words to encourage mommas to know that they are loved by You.

Steven, my dearest husband, thank you for seeing me at my worst and never turning away. You are a true example of forgiveness, reminding me of God's unfailing mercy.

Emma, my sweet girl, thank you for inspiring me to be a better momma so that I can give you the fullest life. I am forever thankful for your bravery, like King David, for facing your giant of type 1 diabetes with grace, and for your ability to love when you could so easily choose not to.

Asher, my precious son, thank you for being a shining light in the darkness.

Delana Sexton, my mother-in-law, thank you for gifting me a journal which led to the becoming of this book. I now have a rare and beautiful treasure to pass down to my children.

Terry Farley, my friend, thank you for sharing your wisdom of writing and encouraging my weary heart to write on.

Damon Davis, my pastor, thank you for shepherding my soul and guiding my writings to become a forty-day journey wrapped up in God's love. I value your wisdom and your time to see this book through.

Brandon and Melodi Hawley, my first inspirations, thank you both for motivating and encouraging this momma to rise early and seek God first. You both planted a seed in my heart and nourished my soul.

Harold Newsome, my former pastor, thank you for initiating the spark in my heart to help mommas know they are loved.

To each and every momma who walked with me on this journey, thank you for your kind words of encouragement and your love that lifted my heart in comfort.

Last but not least, my mother, thank you for building the foundation of Christ in my heart and for your deep desire for me to see His face in glory.

DAY 1

Encouragement

Momma, I am so grateful that you have chosen to be a part of this journey with me! My heart yearns for moms to know how much God loves you. My purpose for this book is to guide you through my real-life mom moments where the enemy tried to defeat me, but God rescued me—moments that I know Mom's face. We are not alone on this journey of raising beautiful children of God who are full of His love and grace.

The moment I realized that God's love is *real* and *alive*, my soul became revitalized with new hope. In the book of Hebrews, the Bible says,

> So there is a special rest still waiting for the people of God. For all who have entered into God's rest have rested from their labors, just as God did after creating the world. So let us do our best to enter that rest. but if we disobey God, as the people of Israel did, we will fall.
>
> *For the word of God is alive and powerful.* It is sharper than the sharpest two-edged sword, cutting between soul and spirit, between joint and marrow. It exposes our innermost thoughts and desires. (Heb. 4:9–12 NLT; emphasis mine)

God has a special rest waiting just for us to enter by the life and power in His word. Through every situation we face, God's word can give us the rest we need because the word is as alive today as it was when Jesus Christ walked this earth. Momma, we all need this rest to be able to raise our little ones to be mighty in Christ! As you read the devotions each day, let His word sink into your soul, knowing that the verses you read are alive and powerful! Let God speak to you through His word and transform you into the mom that He desires you to be. God will do what His word says because "He remains faithful; He cannot deny Himself" (2 Tim. 2:13 NKJV).

Before you begin to read this devotional, take a moment to prepare your heart and mind. There are some choices that I made to better myself and have a closer walk with God that I want to share with you in order to help encourage and strengthen your faith in God. Please note I am not telling you to do exactly what I do; I am just giving you encouragement to start at your pace and grow. These are the things I do every day:

- I encourage you to rise thirty minutes before anyone else in your house is awake and spend some alone time with God. This could be by praying, reading the Bible, and/or reading a devotion. This quiet time with God will open up moments for God to speak life to your heart through His word. Sometimes others may still wake early with you, but attempting this new habit is so worthwhile because your children will see your efforts seeking the Lord in the morning.
- I encourage you to practice reading the Bible, even if you read with audio! Others have encouraged me to read, of which I have found the benefits with reading and seeking the Lord. The more you read, the more you will be able to connect passages with other passages, which will help you throughout your day. Simply reading a verse or chapter a day is a great start! I myself love to read the devotion on the YouVersion Bible app called Bible in One Year. This devotion is a great guideline just to help you read.

- I encourage you to pray for God to help increase your understanding as you read the Bible so that you can teach His word to your children.
- I encourage you to start listening to music that edifies you like contemporary Christian, gospel, or hymns. Reduce or fast secular music and notice the change that takes place by the music you listen to.
- I encourage you to fast something as you read this devotional. You could fast a certain type of food, coffee (Lord be with you!), music, makeup, etc. Maybe even pray and ask the Lord something you need to fast to help improve your life. One of my favorite things to do is go on a social media fast because I allow this to often waste my time and distract me from growing closer to the Lord.

Momma, I hope that you will allow me to encourage you to plant the seed of God's word into your heart. Water and nourish the seed by reading the Bible. The life of His word will grow and flourish in your heart the more you stay connected to Him. We read this in the Word:

> Remain in me, as I also remain in you. No branch can bear fruit by itself; it must remain in the vine. Neither can you bear fruit unless you remain in me. I am the vine; you are the branches. If you remain in me and I in you, you will bear much fruit; apart from me you can do nothing. (John 15:4–5 NIV)

Even Christ says we cannot do anything on our own. We must stay connected to Him to be fruitful. I am praying for you as you take this journey with me. I hope my testimony through these daily devotions will encourage you to take a deeper drink of God's unfailing love freely given to all His children.

DAY 2

In the Beginning

Before I ever became a mother, I attended church faithfully and believed in God. I would read my Bible every now and then and pray when things became hard. I always knew God was our amazing Creator, but I never had that deep connection with Him. Truthfully, I never knew that a connection of love with God ever existed. I thought love consisted of actions like going to church, participating in communion, and doing the right thing. When I did read the Bible, the words didn't sink in deep. I would be a hearer of the word and not a doer of the word. My connection with God wasn't as connected as the relationship needed to be.

When I became pregnant with my daughter, Emma, my heart began to change with the way I felt toward God. I now was not only responsible for my life but for the life of my child. I had the daunting thought that her relationship with God would most likely reflect the relationship I had with God. I realized I needed to change so that I could help guide my daughter through her life. I was encouraged by a pastor to rise up thirty minutes earlier than my usual time every morning and spend that time with God. I would rise early to pray, read my Bible, and ask God to help me understand His word so that I could teach His word to my daughter. Truly seeking God and His wisdom started a spark in my heart that I was excited to keep ignited.

As the time came for my daughter to be born, I was anxious to meet her and see what she looked like. Now, that special bonding moment didn't immediately happen when she entered the world and had her first breath of life, the breath that we use to praise the Lord. Don't get the wrong idea, I did feel happiness because I had finally met my daughter. Yet there were too many distractions that hindered my close connection with her.

The next day, I finally had a moment alone with my precious baby. Our very first moment, just her and I, she started crying; and I had no idea what she needed! I decided I would try to give comfort by rocking her and singing one of my favorite songs "I Won't Give Up" by Jason Mraz. Very soon, my little baby girl stopped crying, and I felt something new—something I had never felt before. Fresh, warm tears started flowing down my face as I sang the verse, "We've got a lot to learn, but God knows we're worth it." In this moment, I questioned, "If I could feel this much love for my child, how much more does God love me?" This new love I was tasting, was it possible that God created me because He loved me this much, honestly, more?

From that moment on, I became hungry and thirsty for God. I wanted to stay wrapped up in His love for me and never let Him go. Even more, I wanted my daughter to know and grow in this love that I now tasted.

A few months later, I discovered that in the book of Genesis, a man named Enoch had a change of heart, just like I did:

> When Enoch had lived 65 years, he became the father of Methuselah. After he became the father of Methuselah, Enoch walked faithfully with God 300 years and had other sons and daughters. (Gen. 5:21–22)

Enoch was the first person mentioned in the Old Testament to have a close walk with God, and it was after the birth of his first child. I like to believe Enoch was just like me and felt that taste of love God has for us through his child Methuselah. God had moved on my heart, just like He had Enoch, and my faith increased even more by knowing this.

Because of this newfound walk with God, I have set my heart to seek God as much as possible, in the bad times and in the good times. I want to completely devote my life to Him and experience the relationship of complete love and joy that God offers. As I seek Him, I desire for all mothers to know that this love isn't just for me but for you too. We are all God's children, and He loves us all the same.

Momma, do you have a moment where you have felt complete joy and love toward someone or something? Reflect on that moment. God gifted to us to experience the emotions we have of love and joy, as well as God Himself feeling love and joy for us. So we can feel love and joy for God too! What a glorious thought knowing that we can have a loving and joyous two-sided relationship with our Heavenly Father!

DAY 3

One More

S ometimes I feel like I am in a season of one more—one more ride in a toy car, one more cookie, one more time down the slide, one more pretzel, the list goes on and on! I tell my daughter Emma "one more" to let her know it is time to call it quits. The other night, as I was reading Emma her bedtime stories, I said, "One more book, and it is time for bed." After the book, she asked specifically for another story, and I said, "I've already said 'one more.'" She then hung her head down but didn't complain. I started thinking, what do I have more important to do than to read her one more story? One day, I won't have the opportunity for the "one more" story, the "one more" song, the "one more" time. I then became teary eyed because I wanted to give my daughter her "one more" due to the love I have for her. So I complied and said, "Okay." Emma lit up and said, "Thank you!"

Sometimes "one more" may be frustrating, but when you think about it, our merciful God is always full of "one more"—one more prayer, one more healing, one more forgiveness. Our God is so full of love for us that He will always help us one more time. The Bible says in Psalms,

> But you, O Lord, are a God of compas-
> sion and mercy, slow to get angry and filled with
> unfailing love and faithfulness. (Ps. 86:15 NIV)

Thank goodness for God's love! This is one of the many examples in the Bible that describes God's love for us. One of my other favorites is found in the Epistle to the Romans:

> No, in all these things we are more than conquerors through him who loved us. For I am convinced that neither death nor life, neither angels nor demons, neither the present nor the future, nor any powers, neither height nor depth, nor anything else in all creation, will be able to separate us from the love of God that is in Christ Jesus our Lord. (Rom. 8:37–39 NIV)

No matter how many times we fail or feel like there is no way God could love us, He still does. Nothing can stop the love of the Lord for us, not even ourselves. As you go through this day, try to remember God is full of "one more" and is ready to pour His love into you. All you have to do is tell Him you need Him in prayer!

DAY 4

For I Love You as Long as the Days

"For I love you as long as the days"—these words leapt off the page and into my heart as I read Emma her bedtime story. We had just spent six very long days with both Daddy and Mommy battling the flu and Emma with strep. My patience was thin, and my energy was depleted.

To beat all, Emma picked the book out to read like she does every night. Her little hands grabbed just the right book that would remind me how much I love her, even when I'm stretched thin.

Previously before the book, I spent a few days barely able to function while I depended on my husband to help us. When I started feeling a little better, my husband took a turn being sick, and now I was the one helping. We both struggled to give Emma the attention we usually do, which led to frustration and a very whiny toddler.

One morning, I desperately needed a moment with God because my temper was ready to fly loose on my toddler's cries of "play with me" repeatedly over and over when I was struggling just to sit up. I snuck away to have a down moment with God to pray and read His word. Proverbs 19:11 struck home as I read the verse multiple times: "A person's wisdom yields patience, it is to one's glory to overlook an offense" (Prov. 19:11 NIV).

That was just what I needed. I immediately prayed for wisdom to deal with Emma's cries and to help me overlook her attitude so

I wouldn't lose my temper. Reacting on her anger with more anger would've been a complete breakdown for the both of us.

Momma, no matter how long the days are, God is still there just waiting for you to search Him in your time of need. Whether it be with sickness, temper tantrums, teenage attitude—God will give you the strength to love during the long days. I know we are human and it is easy to react back with anger, so practice praying this verse before you speak:

> My dear brothers and sisters, take note of this: Everyone should be quick to listen, slow to speak and slow to become angry, because human anger does not produce the righteousness that God desires. (James 1:19–20 NIV)

Remember, you are loved by God more than you will ever know, and He will be there to help you.

DAY 5

Tricky Steps

I am one of those teachers who crosses their fingers for a snow day. Here in West Virginia, we are quite used to the snow—most of the time, to the point where we crave for spring to finally be here. Despite everyone wishing for spring, I am secretly in the corner doing my snow dance with the hopes of a day off to spend with my daughter. On one particular day in mid-March, my snow dance worked, and we received over six inches of snow! My daughter and I were extremely excited for our snow day together so that we could go outside and play.

We decided to go sleigh riding on a very steep hill we have on our property. The path up the hill is extremely rocky, and when you add six inches of snow on top, the conditions are not great for little feet. My daughter Emma was slipping and sliding, as well as I, because we couldn't see where all the rocks were jutting out in the path. Emma was struggling, and I told her to hold onto my hand tight so that I could keep her steady. She jokingly said, "This hill is tricky!" I laughed because I agreed with her.

I couldn't see where I was stepping and was worried about keeping my daughter from falling herself. At one point, Emma wanted to let go of my hand and crawl her way up instead. I told her that crawling would be much harder on her, but her strong-willed two-year-old personality wanted to tackle the hill on her own. She went much slower, snow went inside her boots, and she even started whining about how hard it was to crawl. I ended up carrying her the rest of the way up the hill when she realized that crawling was a very bad idea.

You may be able to see where I am going with this. How often do we as mothers believe that we can carry the load of motherhood on our own? We have a gracious Father willing to hold our hand and keep us steady on the rocky path, but we tend to ignore His help and think we can do it our way. So we do, and we quickly come to realize that our way is so much harder without God guiding us through. We get to the point where we are so beaten down before we even begin to seek God for help, and when we finally do, we are worn plumb out.

Momma, you don't have to let this happen to you! Before you start your day, before you start a new task, and before you guide your child with an important decision—*seek God first!* The Bible says this in the Gospel of Matthew:

> But seek first His kingdom and His righ-teousness and all these things will be given to you as well. Therefore do not worry about tomorrow, for Tomorrow will worry about itself. Each day has enough trouble of its own. (Matt. 6:33–34 NIV)

God wants you to take a hold of His hand so that you do not have to worry about every tricky step that you have to take. When you seek Him first, He will give you what you need for the situation that you are facing. Not only will God supply your needs, but He will bless you too! Psalms reminds us, "Blessed are those who keep His testimonies Who seek Him with the whole heart!" (Ps. 119:2 NKJV).

Wake up in the morning and ask God to guide you through your reading and show you His will. Pray often throughout the day and ask God to lead your footsteps and hold your hand—even if the matter is as simple as asking God for help choosing a healthy dinner that your child will eat. God wants us to come to Him first so that we can be filled with His love and not have to worry. I encourage you to start making a habit of seeking God first, and you will see how much easier your everyday obstacles will become. Remember, Momma, you are loved.

DAY 6

God's Masterpiece

I have always believed that God is the most amazing artist of all time. As an art teacher, I do not believe there is a comparison to the majestic beauties of this world and an artist's rendition of God's work on a canvas. One of my favorite masterpieces by God is the way He paints the morning and night sky. The variety of colors, clouds, and sun rays always captivate me and fill me with a moment where I feel a strong connection with God. I feel His presence when His beauty lights up the sky, so I start to pray for the deepest desires of my heart.

On one particular morning when I was driving to the babysitter before work to drop off my daughter, I was mesmerized by the morning sky. The hues of pink, red, orange, and blue were so breathtaking! I asked Emma to look at the sky and tell me the colors she saw. I proceeded to tell her that God's mercies (His unfailing love) was new every morning and that He painted the sky to remind us of His love. Lamentations 3:22–23 says,

> Because of the LORD's great love
> we are not consumed,
> for His compassions never fail.
> They are new every morning;
> great is your faithfulness. (NIV)

I then proceeded to pray for the deepest desires of my heart. I felt God's love in the sky and gave my worries to Him. I literally was so caught up in communicating with God that I missed our exit! I had to call my boss to let her know I was going to be late and my excuse was, "I was caught up in the beauty of the sky." Yes, I was embarrassed because how often does someone say they were tardy because they were praying? Well, this momma now has.

After I returned my focus to driving, I thought about what just happened. I literally was so caught up in God that I didn't focus on the worries of this world. The thought occurred to me, *What if I lived all day long so caught up in God that His presence filled my heart and the worries of life were lifted away?* Of course, not to the point where you miss your exit and lose focus of your daily life but instead keep yourself wrapped in God's great love to where we aren't consumed by the world. And you know what? I am not the only one who has thought this way! King David thought the same thing in Psalms:

> One thing I ask from the LORD,
> this only do I seek:
> that I may dwell in the house of the Lord
> all the days of my life,
> to gaze on the beauty of the Lord
> and to seek Him in His temple. (Ps. 27:4 NIV)

King David even knew how wonderful living in God's presence was. When storms arise and heartache sinks in, that beautiful love God has to offer is right there waiting for us. God doesn't want us to be consumed with the weight of this world; He wants us to awake fresh in His faithful love and see His beauty.

Momma, please don't let this world consume you. That is exactly what the enemy wants! Try your best to look up above the waves of the storm and keep your eyes and heart on God. When ugliness is all around, search for His beauty. His beauty can be found in the kindness of others, in someone's warming smile, or even a child's innocent laughter. God is faithful, and His love will always surround you.

DAY 7

The Busy Mom

I always love the thrill of the Christmas season and the holiday spirit of joy with giving to others. I enjoy Christmas, even more now that I have a little girl for whom I am able to purchase gifts and see her face light up with excitement. Every Christmas, I start off with enthusiasm and excitement; but by the time Christmas is over, I am exhausted and stressed out.

We have a large family, which means many Christmas visits, much cleaning and preparation, and little time to think about anything else. Every Christmas, I say I am going to do less and enjoy the season, but this last Christmas really took a toll on me. I decided that I needed a break from all the busyness and searched God for His rest.

As I searched for God's rest, I became amazed with how much I make myself busy throughout the whole year and not just during the Christmas season. I jotted down a list of things that made me overwhelmed at times, and this list included cleaning (a big list in itself), cooking, visits with friends, and work. What's worse is that this list of things is necessary for moms to do. We have to do the laundry, sweep, scrub toilets, wipe messy mouths, work, feed our families, and so much more. To top it off, no one usually places much thought with the fact that we make dinner and clean the dishes. We do not receive a certificate for picking up clothes and no award for wiping noses, bottoms, and toilet seats.

The thing is, God sees all that we do. He sees what we do quietly when no one else is watching and no one gives us any credit. We already have His attention simply because of the grace of God and His love for us. As we do our tasks, we can rest in this love and show the same love. We read this in the First Epistle to the Corinthians: "Let all that you do be done with love" (1 Cor. 16:14 NKJV).

All the housekeeping, sports, tasks from work, etc., can be done with God's grace and love instead of with stress. My favorite "busy mom" verse that fills me with peace is from the Epistle to the Colossians:

> Whatever you do, work at it with all your heart, as working for the Lord, not for human masters, since you know that you will receive an inheritance from the Lord as a reward. It is the Lord Christ you are serving. (Col. 3:23–24 NIV)

With every task we have to do, keep in mind that God sees the love we pour out for our family and is not unnoticed. As we serve our family, we are also serving the Lord. Those silly certificates we don't receive for scrubbing a toilet—well, guess what? God will reward us when we do our tasks with love for Him and our family! But I do have one more point to make about being a busy mom.

Sometimes we can become so busy with life and our everyday tasks that we forget or do not make room for time with God. We lay Him on the back burner and make ourselves exhausted trying to do it all without God. Staying focused on our busyness distracts us from the plan God has for us and the rest He has to offer. Spending time without God and staying busy actually depletes us and drains us of life and energy. Don't get me wrong, God does love our work ethic, but when it becomes about doing it all ourselves, then God is not the center of our lives. I read a devotional about this matter, and this saying struck my heart: "If we are too busy for prayer, then we are too busy. If we are too busy to read the Bible, then we are simply too busy."

I believe one of the best circumstances in the Bible about busyness is the story of Martha. Take the time to read the story today in Luke 10:38–42. As Jesus and His disciples were traveling, Martha opened her home to them. As Martha was busy preparing, her sister sat at the Lord's feet, listening to what He said. She let these distractions make her so angry that she whined to Jesus about it and said, "Lord, don't you care that my sister has left me to do the work by myself? Tell her to help me!"

But Jesus gently responded to her that she was letting these distractions worry and upset her. The distractions weren't necessary for Jesus's approval! What was needed more than anything was for Martha to sit at His feet as Mary had chosen. Notice that Jesus did not reply to Martha, "Of course I do care. Mary, go help your sister." But He wanted Martha to come to sit as His feet, spend time with Him, and let the distractions stop bothering her.

In Matthew, we find a rest that Jesus offers when we come to His feet:

> Come to me, all you who are weary and burdened, and I will give you rest. Take my yoke upon you and learn from me, for I am gentle and humble in heart, and you will find rest for your souls. For my yoke is easy and my burden is light (Matt. 11:28–30 NIV)

Instead of being overwhelmed with our busyness, come sit at Jesus's feet and receive His rest. All are invited to Jesus's love, and His way is easier too. When you take Jesus's yoke, He is referring to the yoke that is used to join two animals when they plow to make the burden lighter. He uses this as an example so that you can vision Him helping carry your burden so that you do not have to carry the burden alone. Isn't that amazing? Us moms cannot carry the load by ourselves, and Jesus knows this.

Take the time today to write down what is making you busy and overwhelmed. Sit at Jesus's feet and tell Him your burdens. Let His comfort fill you as you serve your family with love. Let some things go unfinished so that you can spend quality time with your kids.

DAY 8

'Tis the Season

Just the other day, I was gazing outside my classroom window, and I noticed a structure that resembled a goal for a soccer field. Memories came flooding into my mind as I reminisced all the joyful moments I had on the soccer field. Ten years of my life spent learning the game and gaining new friends were memories I will forever cherish. The daydreaming kept going as I thought about high school graduation, my first jobs, and college. I then switched my thinking to my life now. The days of soccer and high school were long past, and my life is now directed toward other things like work, marriage, children, and adult responsibilities. Even though I missed my youth, I enjoyed the thought of where I am now in life, never imagining I would be where I am today.

In each season of my life, there was a purpose, a purpose I could not see and sometimes still can't. Sometimes I made the wrong choices which made life more difficult, not knowing then what the outcome would be. As I look back, I can see God's handiwork in my life and notice why some things happened or did not happen. These moments help me keep my grasp on how real God is because of His appearance in my life. In Ecclesiastes 3:1–8, Solomon points out a lot of circumstances that happen during different seasons. He starts off his thoughts with this: "To everything there is a season, a time for every purpose under heaven" (Eccles. 3:1 NKJV).

There is always a time for something to happen in our lives and a season for us to live in. God wants us to depend on Him in every season so that we can learn to grow into the person we are meant to be. Each season has different trials that we face—some trials we can tackle easier because of what God has already brought us through and some trials we have to learn to fully trust in Him. In each and every season, I encourage you to commit to seeking God and trusting Him to guide us through. We should live wholeheartedly for Him and desire to raise our children to know Him. All this dedication will not go unnoticed either. The apostle Paul says, "And God is able to bless you abundantly, so that in all things at all times, having all that you need, you will abound in every good work" (2 Cor. 9:8 NIV).

I will admit, I do not know how a person survives life without God, especially a mother. There are so many trials and heartaches that are hard to face. Since I have made the time to have a closer walk with God, this season I am going through as a mother is teaching me to lean on God's word all the more. In the seeking, I experience His joy, comfort, peace, and patience so that I am able to make the steps possible to obtain the good work as a mother He calls us for. On the days that feel like they will never end, I have experienced peace and steadiness through the storm instead of worry.

Momma, in this season of motherhood, know that you are not alone! I am not the only mother to know how wonderful our God is. He created each and every one of us to know His love, and He is there to help us through our seasons. Don't let your season be a burden, but let your season be a blessing to you and your children. Remember this verse from the First Epistle of John: "And so we know and rely on the love God has for us. God is love. Whoever lives in love lives in God, and God in them" (1 John 4:16 NIV).

DAY 9

Expectations

We were recently blessed to go on a family vacation and make some great memories. Before I went, I tried not having high expectations with my two-year-old and expectations of a perfectly relaxing vacation. But of course, it is hard to not want a few moments of peace and quiet to yourself so that you can unwind.

On day one of our vacation, Emma ran a high fever, so we spent the day doing the best we could to take care of her. Almost every day, Emma cried to eat chips for breakfast, lunch, and dinner. I even sprayed sunscreen in Emma's eyes because I trusted a two-year-old to close her eyes, and I had to force her to rinse her eyes out at a first-aid station. I may laugh at the situation now, but for two straight hours, Emma cried, which made it difficult to enjoy the day. Eventually, Emma calmed down from every crazy moment and found comfort in Mommy and Daddy, and I couldn't help but be thankful for God blessing me with this little girl and these circumstances to help me learn and grow as a mother.

My patience was tried, my anxiety ran high, and I became worn out. I had to pray, learn to control my temper, help Emma control hers, and find joy in the ugly situations. My thankfulness became stronger when I found joy in the moments where our little girl overcame her tantrums. At the end of our vacation, I read the perfect verse in my daily devotions:

> For our light and momentary troubles are achieving for us an eternal glory that far out-weighs them all. So we fix our eyes not on what is seen, but on what is unseen, since what is seen is temporary, but what is unseen is eternal. (2 Cor. 4:17–18 NIV)

How perfect is that? We all have troubles we face, but God has something so much better for us to fix our eyes on! Oh, of course when the troubles are happening, it is so hard to fix our eyes on the unseen. But we pray, and we don't give up!

I also took the time to watch other mommies and noticed we all face the same troubles where kids test our patience. Emma even noticed crying babies and wanted to pray for them and give them hugs. Momma, when you're in that moment of craziness with your child and see no way out, you have the opportunity to teach your child and bring them closer to God's love. God gave us children for a reason. He picked us to be their mothers and to teach them to know God's heart. No matter where you are, whether it be on vacation, church, dinner, or with family, try not to set your expectations high and keep your eyes fixed on God. He has that eternal glory that far outweighs our momentary troubles.

If I would've had high expectations of a relaxing, stress-free vacation, then my hopes would've been shattered. You have to have the right mindset and realize that having kids means life does not go as planned anymore. Instead of having expectations that every moment will go a certain way, choose to set your mind with being content with the situations you will face. The apostle Paul says in Philippians,

> I am not saying this because I am in need, for I have learned to be content whatever the cir-cumstances. I know what it is to be in need, and

I know what it is to have plenty. I have learned the secret of being content in any and every situation, whether well fed or hungry, whether living in plenty or in want. I can do all this through Him who gives me strength. (Phil. 4:11–13)

According to Google dictionary, *content* means a "state of peaceful happiness." So Paul is saying that in *every* situation, we should be in a state of peaceful happiness. You're probably thinking there is no way to always be happy with every situation. I understand that because some situations in life are more than we can bear. But I believe what Paul is trying to say is not to expect more of the situation, whether good or bad. He even gives away his secret on how to be content in every situation—allow God to strengthen you! So if you are weak in a situation, allow God to fill you with His unsurpassable strength. Tell God you are weak and He is strong and believe that with Him, you will find contentment in every situation.

Momma, I pray you can lay aside your expectations as a mother and the expectations that you have for your children. Find contentment with the trials God is having you go through as a mother and focus on who He is wanting you to become because of those trials. Open up your heart and allow God's strength to carry you through.

DAY 10

Teachable Moment

Let's face it, children are not born knowing how to act perfectly. If they were, then we would have an easy, carefree life, right? Ha! In reality, one of our biggest duties as a mother is to teach our children how to act maturely and become responsible adults. That task is easier said than done, especially when we have our own flaws and pray for our children not to have the same flaws we have.

Now, I admit, I have a hot temper that I've been working on for a while. I have noticed a difference with the way I react toward situations since I have been seeking God, but there are some moments that really test me. For example, my daughter will sometimes overreact to situations and can be very dramatic. She can drop food on the floor, and her temperament will drastically change to a whining tantrum because the food is now dirty. Even worse, sometimes when she doesn't get her way, she will stomp and scream. The screaming triggers an emotion in me and makes by blood boil.

I don't like to admit this, but I immediately want to react in anger and whip her harder than I should. I can even get so mad to the point where I will cry from anxiety and frustration. I have to walk away and shoot a prayer up for help so I can react in God's way, not mine. The apostle Paul says in Ephesians,

> BE ANGRY [at sin—at immorality, at injustice, at ungodly behavior], YET DO NOT SIN; do

not let your anger [cause you shame, nor allow
it to] last until the sun goes down. (Eph. 4:26
AMP)

If we do become angry, we should not stay in that anger. I do
realize how tough it is to control our emotions with our children,
and I also realize that our children learn from our behavior. They
are watching us and soaking everything in. From the TV shows we
watch, the music we listen to, and the conversations we have—our
children are learning from everything we do. It is our responsibility
to teach our children and direct them in the way they should go.
Here's something to ponder from the book of Proverbs: "Start children off on the way they should go, and even when they are old they
will not turn from it" (Prov. 22:6 NIV).

Children will make mistakes, and we can encourage them with
God's word to make the right choices. If we don't teach them cor-
rectly and with God's wisdom, they will grow up to be adults with
temper tantrums; adults who steal; and adults who are dramatic,
envious, hateful, or something else that is not a fruitful spirit.

We can pray and seek God for directions with these teachable
moments. He will provide us with scripture and fill our hearts with
His love. Each and every circumstance we face with our children—
whether it be tantrums, their first heartbreak, or drug and alcohol
addiction—God has encouragement in the Bible that will help us
direct our children in the right way. We have to try our best to lay
aside our fleshly emotions and react wisely. We all make mistakes
with how we react to our children's behavior, but we cannot let each
and every reaction be a mistake. The apostle Paul says, "Make sure
that nobody pays back wrong for wrong, but always strive to do what
is good for each other and for everyone else" (1 Thess. 5:15 NIV).

If a child hits you, don't pay them back with hitting them. If
your child bullies another child at school, don't pay them back with
being a bully to them. If your child tells you they don't love you
in anger, don't say the wrong thing back to them out of anger. Are
you catching my drift? Don't react in the wrong behavior that your
child is exhibiting but react with God's love and word. In Proverbs

22:15, we find that a child's heart has foolishness and that we should administer correction with godly wisdom and loving kindness, not with our emotions:

> Foolishness is bound up in the heart of a child; The rod of discipline [correction admin- istered with Godly wisdom and lovingkindness] will remove it far from him. (AMP)

As your child starts to venture out on their own, they will make mistakes. However, they will always be able to reflect on the teach- able moments they had with you, and those moments will help guide them in the way they should go. Momma, you have the opportunity to give your children God's love as they are growing up and show His love through your reactions and behavior. Observe your lifestyle and reflect on the choices you make and the conversations you have. What do your children see from you? Are you proud of yourself or are you making some mistakes? Make the commitment today and tell God that you choose to teach your child His way, not with your emotions and wrong behavior. Ask for guidance, pray for your child and yourself, and allow God's love to fill your heart so that you can pour that love into your children.

DAY 11

Calling for Rain

Have you ever had one of those days where the forecast was calling for beautiful skies, but your day felt like it was filled with rain? My husband, Steven, just had one of those days. The seal at the bottom of the toilet had busted, so he spent the whole day fixing the problem.

That afternoon, Emma asked for popcorn; and while the popcorn was popping, Steven decided to flush the toilet. Well, there was an unknown clog in the pipe, and poop started shooting up in the shower from the drain! As this was happening, he forgot about the popcorn, and the smoke alarm went off. And to put the icing on the cake, Emma came crying to Daddy that she had a pee accident and peed on the couch. So a poopy shower, burned popcorn, and a pee-stained couch all happened at once, which made the sunny day feel like a downpour on my husband.

Later that evening, Steven read a birthday card from my mom, and she mentioned in the card how Emma always says, "Daddy will fix it," when something becomes broken. The thought humbled him after the catastrophe that had just happened. In our daughter's eyes, Daddy can fix everything, even when Daddy does not have the best of days.

Momma, I know we have all been there and have had these rainy days. The devil sometimes goes to work really hard on us because he wants us to stray away from God's love. He knows how good God is and doesn't want us to have any part of that love. The devil wants us to fix our eyes on the brokenness of this world, on our past mistakes, and not on how God can and will free us from the burden of our problems.

I admit, I have encountered these rainy days, and I have let the enemy win my mind. I have let horrible thoughts fill my mind and turned away from God. I am not proud of those moments and the way I let my family down because of my depression. I used to stay in the depression and never seek a way out. I let the thoughts of doubt and worthlessness become how I was living. I am admitting my faults because I believe other mommas have been in my shoes too and can relate. We also have our own ways of dealing with depression, so I will tell you one of my most memorable breakthrough moments.

This moment of tremendous relief happened to be when I was pregnant with my first child, Emma. I did not want her to know the depression that I knew and the brokenness that I felt. I did not want this depression to become the foundation of her life. So one evening, when I was overcome with horrible thoughts, I dropped to my knees and cried to God. I cried out for the heavy burden to be lifted away and for my daughter to not go through what I was going through. And just like that, I felt the load lift off my shoulders. I felt no more sadness, and my thoughts weren't racing in negativity. I am alive and here today to proclaim that God is alive and truly does help us through our battles!

After this heartfelt moment with God, I strived to be better and seek Him when my thoughts turned negative. I knew God was here to help me, and I searched His Word for help through the battle of depression. I know God lifted my burdens the night I cried out to Him, but I am human and have faced the same crippling thoughts. The enemy knows our weaknesses and does everything in his power to remind us of them. Yet I do my best to practice going to God and training my thoughts to be His thoughts. In Second Epistle to the Corinthians, we find this scripture:

> The weapons we fight with are not the
> weapons of the world. On the contrary, they have

the divine power to demolish strongholds. We demolish arguments and every pretension that sets itself up against the knowledge of God, and we take captive every thought to make it obedient to Christ. (2 Cor. 10:4–5 NIV)

The weapon we can use to demolish the strongholds of bad thoughts is the Bible! Remember, Hebrews 4:9–12 says God's Word is alive and powerful. God's Word, the Bible, can be used to fight back those bad thoughts. If a bad thought brings you down, is negative, and discourages you, then the thought isn't from God. Take captive the negative thought and shut it down.

I have started a habit to find scripture that disagrees with the negative thoughts that race through my mind and write the positive verses on Post-it notes. Whenever the bad thought enters my mind, I pray to God for help and repeat the positive Bible verse. I use God's word to fight against the enemy. I have even memorized a few so that when I am hit hard, I can pray for help and say the Bible verses in my prayer. Let me give you an example. I tend to have anxiety every now and then, so when I am feeling anxious I start to repeat 2 Timothy 1:7: "For God has not given us a spirit of fear, but of power and of love and of a sound mind" (2 Tim. 1:7 NKJV).

I pray to God and tell Him, "Lord, you are the God of power, of love, and of a sound mind. The devil is giving me this fear [anxiety], and I do not want it. I want your peace and guidance through this problem that is causing me anxiety."

Since the night I realized God is hearing my cries to Him, I trust and believe that He will do what His word says He will do. God is faithful and cannot lie (Heb. 6:18). He is the way, the *truth*, and the light (John 14:6). God's word is alive, and all that He says is true. We resist the devil when we speak God's word against the devil's lies. By doing this, the devil will flee from you (James 4:7)! Over time, the devil will realize that you seek God more when he pursues you, and God's peace will start filling your heart where the devils lies used to.

God has been listening to our cries since day one.

> Then they cried to the Lord in their trouble,
> and he saved them from their distress.
> He sent out his word and healed them;
> he rescued them from the grave.
> Let them give thanks to the Lord for
> his unfailing love and his wonderful
> deeds for mankind. (Ps. 107:19–21 NIV)

Notice how the verses say that God sent out His word and healed them. You can literally use God's word to help heal your heartache. He will save you from the death of sin and from suicide. God will pull you out of the grave you are digging yourself into and save you. No matter how bad your rainy day may be, God is just a prayer away.

Momma, I encourage you to Google scripture about the bad thoughts that you have. Maybe you feel insecure as a mother or your children overwhelm you. Maybe you are jealous of other mothers or strive to be perfect. Search God's Word and see what the Bible says about such matters. Write down Bible verses that stick out to you and repeat them throughout your day. Try to memorize one verse at a time and pray the words to God when you're overcome with the negative thoughts. Practice, practice, practice!

Practicing using God's Word to fight the enemy's lies can be compared to practicing something else. Let's say you want to be a better basketball player. In order to become a better player, you have to practice where you are weak. If you are weak with using God's Word, then you have to practice searching and memorizing the verses. Do not get discouraged when the enemy is strong. God is full of compassion and will not give up on you, as we read in Psalms:

> But you, Lord, are a compassionate and gracious God, slow to anger, abounding in love and faithfulness. (Ps. 86:15)

Keep your head up, Momma! We are all in this together, and God wants us to live in His love. I encourage you to use His Word to contradict the enemy's lies and put it into practice!

DAY 12

I Still Love You

We are currently trying to potty train our daughter, and she has been quite resilient. Some days she uses the potty well, and other days she chooses not to. When she has an accident, she will come to either me or my husband with a long, sad face and say that she peed. We then have a discussion with her about the accident, and she will proceed to tell us, "But I still love you." My heart melts when she says this because she knows that she made a mistake and doesn't want us to be angry with her. I tell her, "I will always love you too and that my love doesn't go away. I am just disappointed and trying to teach you how to be a big girl."

Even through potty training, I am given the opportunity to model God's love for my daughter. No matter how many times we mess up, God still loves us. If I stay angry with Emma long after the accident or long after a bad attitude, then I am not reflecting the love God has toward us. I need to be quick to forgive and not hold a grudge. In 1 Corinthians 13:4–8 we find what God's love is and what love is not:

> Love is *patient*, love is *kind*. It does *not envy*, it does *not boast*, it is *not proud*. It does *not dishonor others*, it is *not self-seeking*, it *is not easily angered*, it *keeps no records of wrongs*. Love *does not delight in evil* but *rejoices with the truth*. It

always *protects*, always *trusts*, always *hopes*, always *perseveres*. Love *never fails*. (NIV, emphases mine)

God knows we are human and need to understand His perspective of love. I italicized in the verses what God's love is and what God's love is not. God already loves us this way, and we can learn by His example. Sadly, I think we as humans place rules on how love should be and forget how God loves us. Love is *not* earned; love *is* already given. I believe when we conceive the idea that we have to earn love from people, then we have to earn God's love too. I used to believe that I had to earn God's love through actions. I felt like I had to go above and beyond to please God, just to make Him happy with me. Remember, God is not human. He is our Almighty Creator and a God of compassion. He longs to be gracious to us and will rise up to show us His love (Isa. 30:18 NIV). The book of Jeremiah speaks of God's everlasting love:

> The Lord appeared to us in the past, saying:
> "I have loved you with an everlasting love;
> I have drawn you with unfailing kindness." (Jer. 31:3 NIV)

Everlasting means "lasting forever" or "eternal." That means God's love truly never fails us! According to Reference.com, the King James Version of the Bible mentions God's love 310 times! If love wasn't important to God, then He wouldn't have repeated His love over and over to us. Just think, God loved us so much that He sent His one and only Son to be the ultimate sacrifice for our sins, as we read in the Gospel of John:

> For God so loved the world that he gave His one and only Son, that whoever believes in him shall not perish but have eternal life. For God did not send his Son into the world to condemn the world, but to save the world through him. (John 3:16–17 NIV)

If that isn't love, then I don't know what love could compare to. I cannot even imagine the pain that would rip through my heart if I sacrificed my baby girl for the whole world's sin, especially if my daughter knew no sin like Jesus. Jesus was mocked, ridiculed, beaten, and put to shame; but He never stopped loving. God even knew before He created us that He would sacrifice His Son so that we could spend eternity in Heaven with them, which read in the Epistle to the Ephesians:

> Even before he made the world, God loved us and chose us in Christ to be holy and without fault in his eyes. God decided in advance to adopt us into his own family by bringing us to himself through Jesus Christ. This is what he wanted to do, and it gave him great pleasure. (Eph. 1:4–5 NLT)

God did not want heaven for just Him and Jesus but for all believers in them. He even found pleasure in helping us become a part of His family through His son. God loved us before we even existed. We can somewhat understand this same love if we are given the opportunity to grow our children inside of us or know that we are going to be able to adopt our child. We do not know our child yet, but we are overcome with a great love before we ever lay eyes upon them.

I believe we first need to take root in this great love God has for us so that we can reflect His love to our children. Try to wrap your mind around the fact that *God truly does love you*. He loved us before we existed and allowed His Son to die for our sins so that we could live free in Him. Now, take this love and graciously pour your heart, your soul, and your mind into the Lord and into your children. That is His greatest commandment—to love:

> Teacher, which is the greatest commandment in the Law?"

Jesus replied: "'Love the Lord *your God with all your heart and with all your soul and with all your mind.' This is the first and greatest commandment. And the second is like it: 'Love your neighbor as yourself.'*" (Matt. 22:36–39 NIV; emphasis mine)

If God's greatest commandment is to love, then wouldn't you think that love is quite essential to Him? Love is such a crucial element to have in our lives that Christ gave us a love guideline in First Corinthians. How great is the importance for us to teach this incredible love to our children! Love helps us keep moving forward because without love, we are nothing and gain nothing (1 Cor. 13:1–3).

Momma, as you go through your day and spend time with your children, focus on the endless love God has for you and try to reflect that love to your children. We do not have to earn God's love, so our children should not feel like they have to earn our love. Freely give your children love like God freely gives us His love. When you encounter an obstacle, take a moment to pray for God to guide you in His love. Ask God to remind you of His love in First Corinthians 13 so that you can be patient with your children and slow to anger. Try not to keep a record of their wrongs and show kindness to them. Let them know that you will always love them through the good and the bad, just like God has and will always love us.

DAY 13

The Perfect Mom

If you had to give labels of what the perfect mom looks like, what would you suggest? Would she be put together well, with her makeup on point? Maybe her outfit and her kids' outfits would be completely styled from the most expensive store? Or maybe even her kids always use their manners and listen to their mother?

I've had many moments where I struggled with wanting to be the perfect mom. In my head, I have labeled what a perfect mom should be, and I'm not one of them. I have placed so much burden on my shoulders thinking that every flaw Emma has is my fault and I'm not doing my job as a mother. I even have gotten to the point where I wanted to hide from people so I wouldn't have to worry if they were judging me or not. If I was in public and Emma threw a temper tantrum, I would feel everyone's eyes on me, and I felt like they were thinking that I couldn't control my child. When I couldn't get Emma to show kindness to others, I felt like I did a bad job myself of being the example of kindness she should see. The worst part is when people actually tell me their opinion of what I am doing wrong and that Emma shouldn't act the way that she does. Momma, let me tell you, I beat myself up and bring myself down to an extreme low when I take to heart others' opinions and place an unrealistic burden on my shoulders.

When I get to this point, I end up having to take a step back from my madness so I can quiet myself with God. I have found comfort in so many different ways, through scripture and especially in Emma's eyes. Her eyes hold the depth of so much beauty of who she is and who she can become. I have realized that I need to look at her through God's eyes, not my own. I need to see what He wants me to see and not what society wants me to see. She is developing a personality that matches much of my own, and I have to learn to trust in God so that I can mold these characteristics together to form the child of God that she is meant to be. In the book of Jeremiah, we read, "But blessed are those who trust in the Lord and have made the Lord their hope and confidence" (Jer. 17:7 NLT).

The Lord is where our hope and confidence should be. Our hope and confidence should not be in people's opinions or our crazy ideas of what a perfect mom is. The Lord even blesses us when we place our trust in Him. Through trust and faith, I've learned so much and still have a long way to go. One of my favorite songs I sing to Emma by Jason Mraz says it perfectly: "We've got a lot to learn, but God knows we're worth it." Children aren't born perfect, and neither are mothers. We are learning just as much as they are as we go through each childhood stage. God has such big plans for us, so we need to lay aside our desire to be perfect and trust in Him.

One of the most helpful guidelines in my own personal character as a mother I have found is by conducting and practicing the fruits of the spirit. We read this in Galatians:

> But the fruit of the Spirit is love, joy, peace, longsuffering [patience], kindness, goodness, faithfulness, gentleness, self-control. Against such there is no law. (Gal. 5:22–23 NKJV)

These are the qualities that God hopes for Christians to develop so that we can shine bright for all the world to see! I have had to make quite the effort to practice these fruits by reading devotions, writing scripture, and praying often. But in return, we become the mother that God has always intended for us to be and are modeling His characteristics to our children. Also, the lies that society proclaims of the perfect mom are dismissed by God's truth! When we are living out our lives in God's word, then we have no reason to compare our parenting to others. In His love, we will be made complete and we can overcome the lies of perfection.

Momma, I hope and pray that if you struggle like me, take a moment to look into your child's eyes and see the promise that God holds for them. Look into your own eyes and see the promise that God holds for you as a mother. God chose us for them, and He won't leave us. Don't allow other people's opinions to place unrealistic burdens on your shoulders. Throw out the idea of being the perfect mom and find peace with being a fruitful mom. Go and be blessed as you trust in God's love and practice daily the fruits of the Spirit.

DAY 14

Chosen

In January 2019, I discovered my pregnancy with my second child while Daddy and Emma were cooking dinner and I was secretly waiting in the bathroom to read the pregnancy test. As soon as I saw the positive lines appear, I dropped to my knees and gave praise and thanks to God for blessing me with another child. My favorite mother verse spilled from my lips: "Behold, children are a heritage from the LORD, the fruit of the womb is a reward" (Ps. 127:3 NKJV).

I had inherited another child from God! He rewarded me with another child, and I was humbled and grateful. A few days went by, and I downloaded a baby app on my phone to see what my baby looked like inside my body. At five weeks of life, my baby did not look like a baby. To me, the baby looked like a tadpole, with its head split in half. At first glance of the head not fused together yet, I was reminded of what David had said in Psalms:

> For you created my inmost being;
> you knit me together in my mother's womb.
> I praise you because I am fearfully
> and wonderfully made;
> your works are wonderful,
> I know that full well. (Ps. 139:13–14 NIV)

God was literally knitting my baby together inside of me! Imagine the beauty in God's knowledge to not only know how to form us but to give us different personalities, strengths, weaknesses, likes, dislikes, etc. Even more, He knew my child before I even did! He designed my child from the inside out and had a purpose with His design. What comfort in knowing God specifically designed my child and rewarded me to raise and nurture this child in His love. Now fathom this: God knitted us together too and knew who we were to become, which we read in Jeremiah, "'For I know the plans I have for you,' declares the LORD, 'plans to prosper you and not to harm you, plans to give you a hope and a future'" (Jer. 29:11 NIV)

God has plans for us as mothers and for our children. We are fearfully and wonderfully made with plans to prosper us with a hope and a future. I am filled with awe at how amazing God's love for us is! Momma, if God cares so much about our every detail and our children's, then we obviously have a great purpose as a mother. We are *needed* in God's plan for our children, to raise them to reflect His love. God asks us to do so in Deuteronomy:

> Love the Lord your God with all your heart and with all your soul and with all your strength. These commandments that I give you today are to be on your hearts. Impress them on your children. Talk about them when you sit at home and when you walk along the road, when you lie down and when you get up. (Deut. 6:5–7 NIV)

I yearn to seek God more and to love Him with all my heart, soul, and strength. He spent so much time knitting me together and planning my life that He deserves for me to dedicate my heart to Him. God rewarded us with our children, so why not raise them to know of His love? I mean, if you think about it, the love that we feel toward our children is just a taste of the love that God feels toward us. The Bible even says so, "We love because He first loved us" (1 John 4:19 NIV).

Momma, God blessed us with these children and with this love. Let us choose to give back that love to God and raise our children, knowing how much they are loved by us and by God.

DAY 15

Build Them Up

Since we are adding a new child to our family, my husband has been hard at work building an extra bedroom onto our house to make room. Thankfully, we are blessed enough to add on, and my husband even spoiled my daughter and I by building us an art room! I'm pretty sure every artist dreams of their own little studio, so I am pretty ecstatic about the new addition.

Now, I have no clue where to begin when it comes to doing the math and the layout of a home, but my husband has had the education needed to lay out and build the extra rooms onto the house. He is wise in his field and is fully knowledgeable in building a house with a strong foundation. On the other hand, you have me—all giddy like a kid on Christmas morning, excited to fill the rooms with baby furniture and art supplies!

As my husband has been building onto our home, I read some Bible verses that made me think of him, specifically this verse from Proverbs:

> By wisdom a house is built,
> and through understanding it is
> established; through knowledge its
> rooms are filled with rare and
> beautiful treasures. (Prov. 24:3–4 NIV)

My husband has the wisdom and understanding to build onto our home, but when I read these verses, I considered them in a different context. I see these verses referencing people as building their homes wisely in the Lord and having their children built up wisely in the Lord. The beautiful and rare treasures are not valuable possessions, but they are the memories made and your child's heart filled with God's love. You can have the biggest house and the most expensive possessions, but these things are worthless when it comes to our salvation. When we build our homes, we should build our homes with God's love. Only then will we see our treasures unfold in our children as they exhibit the knowledge of God. Teaching our children the words of the Bible is the most precious treasure that we could ever gift to our children. In Second Timothy, we find this piece of scripture:

> All scripture is God-breathed and is useful for teaching, rebuking, correcting, and training in righteousness, so that the servant of God may be thoroughly equipped for every good work. (2 Tim. 3:16–17 NIV)

All of God's Word is useful for guiding our children. What a massive book of instruction that we can use to guide us! I have always joked that I wish children came with a manual, but thankfully, the Bible is a guide that we can use to teach them wisely and equip them for every good work they will do in the Lord. In Colossians, we find a great verse of how mothers can clothe themselves with God's example and start building their children up: "Therefore, as God's chosen people, holy and dearly loved, clothe yourselves with compassion, kindness, humility, gentleness and patience" (Col. 3:12 NIV).

Before the apostle Paul even tells us how to clothe our temperaments, he lets us know how loved we are by God. We are His chosen people, holy and dearly loved. Since God loves us so much, He will help us clothe ourselves with the traits He wants us to exhibit. When we exhibit these traits to our children, we are expressing God's love and equipping them for their future. Truthfully, a person who is compassionate, kind, humble, gentle, and patient is someone we would much rather be around than someone who is hateful, mean, and quick to anger. Start your children off right by building the Godly traits into their hearts.

In the Gospel of Luke, Jesus describes a parable of the two foundations:

> As for everyone who comes to me and hears my words and puts them into practice, I will show you what they are like. They are like a man building a house, who dug down deep and laid the foundation on rock. When a flood came, the torrent struck that house but could not shake it, because it was well built. But the one who hears my words and does not put them into practice is like a man who built a house on the ground without a foundation. The moment the torrent struck that house, it collapsed and its destruction was complete. (Luke 6:47–49 NIV)

This parable ties in perfectly with today's devotion. A house cannot stand on weak foundation, just like we cannot stand without building our lives on Christ, our rock. We will easily fall when storms come into our lives if we live without Christ. The importance of building a strong foundation in Christ now is critical so when we do face a raging storm, we will have a sturdy foundation with Him by our side. The torrent will strike our lives but will not be able to shake our faith if we are well built in Christ and put His words into practice.

Momma, all the hard work and efforts will pay off because God's love never fails. The Word in Deuteronomy says this:

> Know therefore that the Lord your God is God; He is the faithful God, keeping his covenant of love to a thousand generations of those who love him and keep his commandments. (Deut. 7:9 NIV)

He keeps His covenant of love with those who are faithful to the next generation. How comforting it is to know that the effort we make to teach our children of God will not go unnoticed!

We may not have a children's manual to guide us on how to raise our children, but we do have God's love and His Word that is full of life. I pray the Lord will lead and guide us as we teach His concepts to our children. When the storms come and beat upon our faith, our sturdy foundation in Christ will help protect and strengthen us against the evil from the devil.

Momma, I encourage you to build your children up on Christ, the rock, and clothe them with His loving traits. Your efforts will not go unnoticed, and your home will be filled with the glorious treasure of seeing your children have God's gracious love abounding in their hearts.

DAY 16

Faith Through the Storm

The day had begun just as normal as any typical day started in our household. I was nineteen weeks pregnant and allowed Emma to choose her breakfast, which was leftover pizza. After she had eaten, she became extremely tired, even though she had just slept over twelve hours. She didn't want to play but wanted me to carry her around everywhere through the house. As I carried Emma on top of her growing brother, I noticed that her breathing was labored. Her previous symptoms from the past few weeks of excessive thirst didn't really faze me because I just assumed she was a healthy, thirsty three-year-old. But now with no energy and the labored breathing, I knew something wasn't right. I called the doctor for an appointment, and miraculously there was one opening with only one doctor at the facility.

I had a feeling Emma might have had high blood sugar because of her excessive thirst, so I asked the nurse to check her blood and her urine. The nurse checked her urine and pricked Emma's finger. After checking the blood sample on the glucometer, she left the room immediately without saying a word. The doctor came into the room and asked me to tell her why I was here and what Emma's symptoms were. She then looked at me with eyes I will never forget. Her eyes were full of sympathy. I could see in her eyes that she knew the sorrow we were about to face, and in the gentlest voice possible, she said, "Emma's blood sugar was too high to read, so you need to take her to the hospital immediately."

I had a million questions and she answered everyone with the utmost love, but fear gripped my heart. I was not allowed to let her eat lunch or take a nap. I did not understand at the time, but Emma could have entered a diabetic coma in her sleep.

The whole way to the hospital, I found comfort with my mother-in-law. We listened to praise-and-worship music while trusting and believing that God had everything in control, especially since the doctor's appointment had been available. When we arrived, the emergency team immediately received Emma into their care, rechecked her blood glucose that was still over five hundred, and admitted her into a room. The staff were so incredibly brilliant and perfect with my daughter! I will never forget their kindness and love they shown her and my family. Upon placing an IV in her arm, they drew blood to run tests. I had no clue what was going on, but I felt wrapped up in God's love and tried my best to reassure my daughter.

Finally, the doctor came to my family and informed us that Emma had type 1 diabetes (T1D) and was in diabetic ketoacidosis (DKA). If we had not brought her in when we did, she would have only survived one more week! Not fully understanding the situation, I asked the doctor, "What do we need to do to fix this illness and take care of our daughter?" And I will never forget his response: "She has an autoimmune disease, and there is no known cure as of now. You did nothing to cause this either, but her body attacked her insulin-producing cells, and now her pancreas will no longer produce insulin, which helps the cells absorb the glucose in her body. We don't know what causes type 1 diabetes either."

My mind drew a blank. I did not know how to perceive this unimaginable information. I still had faith in God that He would take care of my daughter, but my mind raced with the question *why*, why is my daughter—the healthy, vibrant three-year-old—stricken with an illness that is not found on either side of our family? Why my beautiful, precious little girl? I pondered these questions and cried them out to God later in prayer.

Emma stayed in the PICU unit of the hospital for two days. While we were there, we were educated just enough to be able to take Emma home for a week and return for a more thorough education the following week. We were taught the basics of type 1 diabetes, how to calculate and administer inulin, how to count carbs, how to check blood glucose, how to check ketones in her urine, and what to do if an emergency low happened—a low that would send her into a coma and then death if we did not administer glucagon quick enough. The word *overwhelmed* was an understatement.

After a total of four long days in the hospital, we were finally able to go home and adjust to our new lifestyle. My husband immediately threw all the candy and junk food in our home into the trashcan, while I tried to organize all of Emma's new medical supplies. As I was storing the supplies, I noticed a drawing with a Bible verse I had drawn two days before Emma was diagnosed with T1D. I had experienced a sleepless night, and an image of a tree full of life, with its roots wrapped around God's heart, would not leave my mind. So I decided to rise and draw the picture. I reread the verses that went with the drawing:

> I pray that out of his glorious riches he may strengthen you with power through his Spirit in your inner being, so that Christ may dwell in your hearts through faith. And I pray that you, being rooted and established in love, may have power, together with all the Lord's holy people, to grasp how wide and long and high and deep is the love of Christ, and to know this love that surpasses knowledge—that you may be filled to the measure of all the fullness of God. (Eph. 3:16–19 NIV)

Was God preparing me for something far greater than I could ever possibly understand? He knew what we were about to face and placed this image with these verses in my thoughts, wrestling me through the night, to hear His calling. Was He truly giving me encouragement to stay wrapped up in His love on the new journey our family was about to face? Could God be possibly calling me deeper into His love that surpasses my understanding? The answers did not come that night, but slowly and steadily, they came piece by piece through the last devotions in this book. My whole perspective of God's love became torn and resewn together in a journey of suffering and keeping faith through the storm.

Momma, I pray that through the next several days, your heart will be opened up to God's love even deeper than you ever thought possible. I encourage you to take the time to pray too, to be able to grasp how wide and long and high and deep the love of Christ is so that you may be filled to the measure of all the fullness of God.

DAY 17

Even If

Inspired by the song "Even If" by MercyMe

One week, I was extremely down over Emma's diabetes and wanted to give up. I was tired of thinking of all I had to do for her diabetes and not enjoying anything about my new unborn child.

During this discouraging week, I read Emma's children's Bible to her, and one of the stories told of Jesus healing a woman who touched His coat and a blind man who gained his sight when Jesus placed mud in his eyes. After the stories, I gave insulin to my mad, crying child and sat down to read my Bible devotion, crying myself. I was filled with anger and hurt, super mad at God, and I cried out in prayer, questioning His power of not healing my daughter even when I knew He could.

I then opened my Bible to read my devotion, and God came through, even though I was mad with Him and just questioned His power. The story I read was about Shadrach, Meshach, and Abednego in Daniel 3:13–30. These men wouldn't worship King Nebuchadnezzar's gods or the image of gold he made. The king questioned them and threatened to burn them in a furnace. Here was their response:

> "If we are thrown into the blazing furnace,
> the God we serve *is able* to deliver us from it, and

he will deliver us from Your Majesty's hand. But *even if he does not*, we want you to know, Your Majesty, that we will not serve your gods or worship the image of gold you have set up." (Dan. 3:17–18 NIV; emphasis mine)

The men knew God was able to deliver them from death, but *even if He didn't*, they still wouldn't turn their back on God. Even through their proclamation of faith, they were still thrown into the furnace. King Nebuchadnezzar was so furious with them that his attitude changed and he ordered the furnace to become *seven* times hotter. So hot that the soldiers who threw Shadrach, Meshach, and Abednego into the fire died from the heat! This hotter furnace reminds me that the devil gets mad when we don't give up on God and tries even harder to hurt us, just like King Nebuchadnezzar tried ever harder to hurt the faithful men.

Miraculously, King Nebuchadnezzar was shocked when he saw not three but four men walking in the fire unharmed and the fourth like the Son of God. We continue reading,

Then King Nebuchadnezzar was astonished; and he rose in haste and spoke, saying to his counselors, "Did we not cast three men bound into the midst of the fire?"

They answered and said to the king, "True, O king."

"Look!" he answered, "I see four men loose, walking in the midst of the fire; and they are not hurt, and the form of the fourth is like the Son of God." (Dan. 3:24–25 NKJV)

Even when we can't see Jesus, He is walking with us through the fire (trial) and we are not consumed by the flames. Because of the three men's faith, the king's faith and his attitude toward God changed. He brought the men out of the fire, promoted them, and proclaimed to the people that no other god can save in the way the three men were saved! The flames hadn't even touched them, even though the soldiers who threw them in died from the heat.

Momma, I encourage you to keep the faith during this fiery ordeal of a trial. God is walking beside you *even if* He isn't doing what we know He can do. The devil is working harder to break us because the devil knows that our continued faith in God will help change others, just like King Nebuchadnezzar. Whatever your circumstance is, proclaim to the devil that *even if God does not* heal the circumstance you are facing, you *will not* give up on God. God may not deliver us *from* the trial, but He will deliver us *through* the trial.

DAY 18

I'm Right Here with You

Some days are completely and utterly exhausting. On one particular day, I had little sleep and was overwhelmed with counting my daughter's carbs, checking her glucose, administering insulin corrections, and seeing consistently high blood sugar due to her type 1 diabetes. I had been so focused and stressed about trying to be perfect so that Emma's glucose numbers would be right that I quit taking care of myself. I needed to cry, so I kept the tears back until she couldn't see me cry. I wanted to be strong for my little girl, but I didn't feel like I was.

Later that day, we had to take our dog, Sky, to the veterinarian for a checkup. I told Emma that we have to help Sky not be scared of her shots and be brave like her when she gets her shots of insulin. While we were in the waiting room, Sky started howling because she was anxious. Emma wrapped her arms around Sky in a big hug and said, "Don't worry, Sky, I'm right here with you." And I broke. Those were the exact words I used to comfort my daughter in the hospital when she was diagnosed with type 1 diabetes. The doctors had to draw her blood every hour all night long to make sure her glucose levels were decreasing slowly in order for her brain to not swell. Every time she woke up to the nurse drawing her blood from her IV, she would cry in fear, so I would wrap my arms around her and say, "Don't worry, Emma, I'm right here with you." Little did I know, she was soaking up what I was saying and absorbing my comfort.

Then the thought dawned on me—God has seen me over-whelmed, tired, and crying in exhaustion. He must be doing the same for me by wrapping His arms around me and saying, "*Don't worry, my child, I'm right here with you.*" The Old Testament even says He will never leave us:

> "Be strong and courageous. Do not be afraid
> or terrified because of them, for the LORD your
> God goes with you; *he will never leave you nor
> forsake you.* (Deut. 31:6 NIV; emphasis mine)

In the New Testament, the writer of the book of Hebrews references back to the same verse: "Never will I leave you; never will I forsake you" (Heb. 13:5 NIV).

Through all the tears, the Lord our God is right beside us, holding us tight. Imagine all that you do for your child or someone you love, to give them comfort through their worries, their fears, and their tears—now realize that God does the same for you through your worries, fears, and tears. Rest in comfort today that He is right there beside you, holding you tight and whispering, "Don't worry, my child, I'm right here with you."

DAY 19

Peace Over Fear

Have you ever felt like you were looking at the winds in the storm and not keeping your focus on Jesus? All you could see was disaster ahead and not the peace that Jesus has to offer. This reminds us of the moment when Peter saw Jesus walking on the lake coming toward the boat he was in. Peter wanted to come to Jesus in the water, but when he saw the wind was strong, he began to sink! He took his eyes off Jesus and allowed his fear to overcome him. You can find this story in Matthew 14:22–33.

It is very easy to take our eyes off Jesus when stressful moments happen in our lives. One morning, I read this verse: "I am leaving you with a gift—peace of mind and heart. And the peace I give is a gift the world cannot give. So don't be troubled or afraid" (John 14:27 NLT).

I had been overcome with fears lately, mainly fears with Emma's new diabetes diagnosis, so I decided to write down every fear I had:

- fear of her sugar levels dropping or being too high,
- fear if she was eating the right amount of carbs,
- fear of eating at the perfect time between meals,
- fear that her sugar will drop in the night and I won't wake up in time,

- fear of not drinking enough water and having ketones in her urine,
- fear of her developing resentment toward me giving her insulin shots,
- fear of me being too harsh on her,
- fear of her being sleepy as a sign of high blood sugar,
- fear if I am doing everything right,
- fear of being able to find low-carb foods,
- fear of crying in front of her or others when I am supposed to be strong,
- fear that she will see candy at the store,
- fear of others wanting to give her food that doesn't fit into her carb amount,
- fear of not knowing how to calculate treats into her carb amount, especially when she deserves them, and
- fear of eating food in front of her because she might want some...so I hide.

Whoa, is that a list of fears or what? I literally wrote down all these fears and teared up because I was letting so much fear consume me. To beat all, I did not even write down my fears of parenting, working, and a new child on the way. I realized there was no reason for me to keep allowing these fears to consume me, so I started to pray and give each fear to God with this verse:

> But I called on your name, Lord,
> from deep within the pit.
> You heard me when I cried, "Listen to my pleading!
> Hear my cry for help!
> Yes, you came when I called;
> you told me, *"Do not fear."* (Lam. 3:55–57 NLT)

Like this verse says, I cried to the Lord from deep within my fears and allowed myself to hear Him say, *"Do not fear."* I asked for help because God will hear us and tell us we do not have to be scared, just as we read in the Word:

> Don't worry about anything; instead, pray about everything. Tell God what you need, and thank him for all he has done. Then you will experience God's peace, which exceeds anything we can understand. His peace will guard your hearts and minds as you live in Christ Jesus. (Phil. 4:6–7 NLT)

All those fears I was able to tell God about so that I could receive His *peace.* Even though it is hard to thank God for Emma's situation with type 1 diabetes, I took a long look at my daughter and thanked God for choosing her for me. I thanked God for the love I have in my heart for her and my desire to help her through the obstacles of type 1 diabetes with grace. After I prayed, I felt that *peace* that exceeded my understanding overcome me and guard my heart and mind.

Maybe you have a child with an illness and can relate to some of my fears that I listed. Maybe you have a completely different list of fears that no one knows about. Write them down. Read each one to God in prayer, ask for help, and give thanks for the help He is going to provide you. If you have a church that does altar calls, you can take your list of fears to the altar and lay them at Jesus's feet. The bold movement could help even more with releasing your fears so that you can feel the Lord's perfect *peace.* Try to realize all the efforts we make to help our children overcome their fears and obstacles, God helps us even more with our own fears. I pray you can be filled with God's perfect *peace* and can overcome the fear that the devil wants to place in your heart.

DAY 20

Be Still

One morning as I started to journal my thought process, I was redirected toward a different perspective: "The Lord will fight for you; you need only to be still" (Exod. 14:14 NIV).

This Bible verse was my Bible app's daily verse, and when I read the verse, I thought of my fight to keep Emma alive because Steven and I are her pancreas. But this verse reminds me that God is in control. Even though her pancreas's insulin productions have stopped and we have to administer insulin, God did provide doctors with the intelligence to create insulin so that people with T1D can live today. Before insulin existed, the only way to survive T1D was through starvation, and then you eventually starved to death. So if God has allowed us to come this far, how much farther will He go? I only have to be still and allow Him to fight this battle.

We find this wonderful story in 2 Kings 6:15–17 about a servant of Elisha who was filled with fear because they were surrounded by an army of horses and chariots:

> And when the servant of the man of God arose early and went out, there was an army, surrounding the city with horses and chariots. And his servant said to him, "Alas, my master! What shall we do?"

So he answered, "Do not fear, for those who *are* with us *are* more than those who *are* with them." And Elisha prayed, and said, *"LORD, I pray, open his eyes that he may see* [my italics]." Then the Lord opened the eyes of the young man, and he saw. And behold, the mountain *was* full of horses and chariots of fire all around Elisha. (2 Kings 6:15–17 NKJV)

Notice that Elisha said in verse 16, "Do not fear, for those who are with us are more than those who are with them." Elisha prayed for his eyes to be opened to see the Lord's mighty army instead of the human army.

How easy it is to look at the battles in front of us instead of seeing what God is doing for us. I tend to look at Emma's blood glucose numbers, the highs and lows, and her snack/meal carb amount and allow these things to consume me. Just like Elisha's servant, I see the human battle before me and not what God's army is doing for me. This passage reminds me that when the battles start to consume me, I need to start praying that the Lord will open my eyes that I may see Him and not this disease.

Whenever something starts to cause fear inside of you, remember to stop and pray to not see the problems lying in front of you but ask God to open your eyes to see the Lord fighting for you. The Lord is always fighting for us—we need only to *be still.*

DAY 21

Temptation

Did you know Jesus was tempted? So much so that He was filled with deep sorrow and cried to God in prayer. We read this in the Letter to the Hebrews:

> "For we do not have a high priest who is unable to empathize with our *weaknesses*, but we have one who has been tempted in every way, just as we are—yet he did not sin. Let us then approach God's throne of grace with confidence, so that we may receive mercy and find grace to help us in our time of need" (Heb. 4:15–16 NIV; emphasis mine)

Jesus went through struggles just like us, so He knows how to empathize with our weaknesses. Because of His suffering, we can use His example to approach God and find grace to help us in our time of need.

So what is Jesus's example to find God's grace? We read this in Hebrews:

> During the days of Jesus' life on earth, he offered up *prayers* and petitions with fervent *cries* and tears to the one who could save him from

death, and he was heard because of his reverent
submission [to God's will]. Son though he was,
he learned obedience from what he suffered.
(Heb. 5:7–8 NIV; emphasis mine)

Did you catch that? He submitted to God's will and prayed so
deep with cries and tears that God heard Him. Even God's own Son
suffered tremendous pain, and because of this pain, he learned obedience. Jesus suffered because He had to carry such a great burden
of being a sacrifice for our sins! Jesus needed help and went to pray
right before it was time for Him to be crucified, and you can find this
story in Luke 22:39–46 and Matthew 26:36–46. Jesus was so deep
with sorrow that his sweat was like drops of blood. Jesus even asked
His disciples to pray too so that they wouldn't fall into temptation,
but they fell asleep on Him!

I imagine that Jesus could have been filled with the temptation
of anger because of His disciples' doubts, lack of self-control, and
even jealousy that He had to bear the weight of the world's sin and
no one else did. But God heard His cries and sent an angel to give
Him strength through the suffering—the suffering through Judas's
betrayal, His disciples deserting Him, and the pain up on the cross.

Jesus loved us so much that He didn't give up. He fought
through the temptation, not only to be a sacrifice for our sins but to
help teach us obedience to God's will during our suffering. Whatever
we are suffering, whatever fills us up with deep sorrow—remember
to cry out to God in prayer like Jesus did. God will strengthen you
through the hurt and guard your hearts against the temptations you
will face.

DAY 22

Burdens

As I watched Emma sleep peacefully in her tent, I thought about all the efforts that I make to allow her to have that sweet sleep. Emma can't take care of herself and check her blood glucose, count her carbs, give herself shots, call the doctor with her blood glucose numbers, work to pay for her insulin, or watch the clock to keep herself on a schedule. Even more, I try my hardest to not allow her to feel burdened by the autoimmune disease. I want my daughter to *not* have a lifestyle of illness but one of prayer, bravery, seeking the good, and remembering to be little. Quite often I have to remind myself that Emma is three years old, not an adult. She is a toddler *full of life* that should thrive on being little, not grown-up. I try my hardest to allow Emma to keep the joy in life and not the sadness that an autoimmune disease can bring.

I carry all this burden so that she doesn't have to. And with that thought, I remembered this verse: "Carry each other's burdens, and in this way you fulfill the law of Christ" (Gal. 6:2 NIV).

When she is down, I do my best to bring her up. I make the effort to pray with her and think positively so that she can keep living life to the fullest and not on the edge of despair. Carrying her burdens and my own has become so heavy at times that I feel like I am made completely of glass, hovering on the edge of a cliff and at any moment, I will fall off and shatter into a million pieces. *But I don't have to feel that way.*

If you continue reading in Galatians, you'll find encouragement: "Let us not become weary in doing good, for at the proper time we will reap a harvest if we do not give up" (Gal. 6:9 NIV).

I DO HAVE A CHOICE! I could give up and run out on my daughter, allowing myself to become shattered from the burdens, or I could allow God to sustain (strengthen or support) me and look forward to the harvest at the end of this journey. "Cast your burden on the LORD, And He shall sustain you; He shall never permit the righteous to be moved," we read in Psalms 55:22 (NKJV).

Sustain—let that word sink in. When you give your burdens to the Lord, He will sustain you by strengthening and supporting you. You don't have to live on the edge of a cliff just waiting for the moment that you will fall into despair and break. God will sustain you through all the burdens as you cast them all upon Him as He says in the Gospel of Matthew,

> "Come to me, all you who are weary and burdened, and I will give you rest. Take my yoke upon you and learn from me, for I am gentle and humble in heart, and you will find rest for your souls. For my yoke is easy and my burden is light." (Matt. 11:28–30 NIV)

God's will and way is much easier than trying to handle all the burdens on our own. We add burdens on our shoulders and make the load unbearably heavier than we should. We are not meant to carry all the weight on our own. When we carry each other's burdens or our children's burdens, God will carry our burdens too. They will find rest with our help, as well as us finding rest with God's help. He sustains us, and we can help show that same love and sustain our children.

Momma, take a moment today and literally lay each burden at the Lord's feet. Speak to God in prayer, place that burden in your hands, and drop it off at the Lord's feet. Allow your shoulders to be lightened as you give your burdens away to take up the Lord's easy yoke and follow His will for your life.

DAY 23

God's Timing

I'll admit, I had let go of the thought of me being pregnant and stopped thinking of another blessing coming my way. Emma's new diagnosis literally consumed my every thought, and the joy of a newborn left me. So one day, I started thinking about the timing of Emma's new brother and her diagnosis with type 1 diabetes. I actually grew thankful that the baby wasn't here yet so that we could get a small grasp on Emma's new lifestyle. I then remembered that I actually prayed for the little boy to be here sooner than he is going to be, and now I see God's timing for our son in full circle.

When I wanted to be pregnant, I would've had this baby right when Emma was diagnosed. I could've missed her symptoms by being overwhelmed with a newborn and even more stressed out learning her new diet and insulin routine. Now I can see why God didn't allow me to be pregnant when I wanted to be. He was listening to my prayers, even when I thought He wasn't. He knew what was going to lie ahead for our family and made things work out for us in *His timing*. Psalms 130:5 reminded me, "I wait for the Lord, my soul waits, And in His word I do hope" (KJV).

I actually took a step back before I was pregnant and submitted to God's will, even though I didn't know what His will would be. Seeing His plan for our son's timing come full circle fills me with much more peace knowing He is in control of Emma's diabetes and helping our family every step of the way. So as I pondered God's timing for this little boy, I enjoyed being pregnant again. This verse helped me in hoping for the good in God's timing:

> "The Lord is my portion," says my soul,
> "Therefore I hope in Him!"
> The Lord *is* good to those who wait for Him,
> To the soul *who* seeks Him.
> *It* is good that *one* should hope and wait quietly
> For the salvation of the Lord. (Lam. 3:24–26 NKJV)

Like I did before I was pregnant, I need to take a step back again and submit to God's will—this time, in the waiting with type 1 diabetes. Who knows how long Emma will have to endure the hardships of the disease or if there will ever be a cure? But we can hope in the Lord during our waiting and seek His face through all the highs and lows. Finding the Lord in the waiting strengthens our hearts and minds, which helps us grow to be more like Jesus and less like ourselves. The outcome after the waiting is more beautiful than if we rush to find the end. Pastor Damon Davis of New Life Tabernacle spoke of this waiting well and referred to Psalms 37:23–24:

> The steps of a good man are ordered by the Lord, and He delights in his way. Though he fall, he shall not be utterly cast down; For the LORD upholds him with His hand. (NKJV)

God has a destiny for us and a place He wants us to be. We walk in the waiting on God's plan because God is ordering our steps to get us to His outcome. The process through the journey gives us strength as we pray and seek Him. The steps the Lord orders for us aren't going to be of perfect situations, but with obstacles and trials. But we won't be utterly cast down as we walk the steps ordered by the Lord. He will uphold us with His hand (sustain us) along the way.

God doesn't want us to wait on His timing by ourselves. He knows life is hard because even Jesus lived the hard life in the flesh.

The Lord wants us to come to Him with our problems. He won't reject us but will be good to us. Even though it is hard to wait in our "instant gratification" world, we have to wait on His timing and His plan. But the wait will be worth the process because there is strength in the waiting:

> Wait on the LORD;
> Be of good courage,
> And He shall strengthen your heart;
> Wait, I say, on the Lord! (Ps. 27:14 NKJV)

Not only will your heart be strengthened in the waiting, but your strength will also be renewed, as we read in Isaiah:

> But those who hope in the Lord
> will renew their strength.
> They will soar on wings like eagles;
> they will run and not grow weary,
> they will walk and not be faint. (Isa. 40:31 NIV)

We will be able to go the distance with the Lord and not grow weary because of the Lord's strength. *Waiting* means to have patience, longsuffering, and delaying action for the Lord's timing. We wait with the Lord for the hope of the plan He has in store for us because we have to be prepared for what He needs us to be. And while we go through our time of waiting, we can grow in our journey of becoming closer to the Lord.

Momma, I pray we keep our eyes on the steps the Lord is ordering for us and to not live in disappointment, wishing to be rushed to the end of the obstacles we face. Let our hearts be strengthened and renewed as we wait and hope on the Lord. We get the chance to build ourselves and our children up into who God wants us to be as we wait for *His timing*.

DAY 24

Grace

Let us then approach God's throne of *grace*
with confidence, so that we may receive
mercy and find *grace* to help us in our time of need.
(Heb. 4:16 NIV, my emphasis)

On one of the many sleepless nights I experienced with a type 1 diabetic and a newborn, the enemy was strongly trying to bring me down in my tired mind. I was thinking selfishly about "me, me, me" and was overcome with exhaustion. I had been praying lately for God's grace and help, and during this particular night of highs and lows in my daughter and a hungry, congested newborn, God's grace found me in my time of need.

I started thinking about storms and questioned myself, "What do we do when a thunderstorm is about to happen?" When we see the dark clouds rolling in and the lightning about to strike, we take shelter and run inside to stay safe. If there is an earthquake, hurricane, or tornado, what does the news station always warn us to do? Seek safety! We go through different safety measures to protect us and our loved ones. And sure enough, the storm will always pass.

Now, what do we do if our child becomes sick? We do everything we can to take care of them and keep them safe. We take them to the doctor, if need be, to give them the most protection. But what happens when the doctors give a diagnosis of illness that the child will have to face for a very long time or the rest of their lives? The storm they are going to face doesn't pass like a thunderstorm does or a hurricane, earthquake, and a tornado. The storm is a constant, ongoing battle of highs and lows. So who do we seek for help with this storm, the storm that feels like it will never come to pass?

In Psalms 18:1–2, you can find verses of David singing to the Lord the day the Lord rescued him from Saul:

> I love you, LORD;
> you are my strength.
> The Lord is my rock, my fortress, and my savior;
> my God is my rock, in whom I find protection.
> He is my shield, the power that saves me,
> and my place of safety. (NLT)

There you have it! A beautiful ray of hope through the dark clouds. In the Lord we have strength, a sturdy rock to stand on, a fortress of protection, and a Savior! He shields us from the elements, has the power to saves us, and in Him we are kept safe. *The most reliable hope we have of making it through our storms in life is with Jesus Christ, our Savior.* Through the grace of Jesus Christ, He willingly died on the cross to bring salvation to all people. Everyone has the opportunity of a heavenly home and to experience Christ's love.

Every time you feel like the storm is going to swallow you up, God's grace is right there, ready to carry you through. By the grace of God, we are saved *every single time*! Even through all the suffering, heartache, and pain, God's grace is still there.

When we feel like the waves have knocked us down and we are drowning, the Lord will rescue us.

When there seems to be no way and all is lost, God's love still shines through.

When we can't see past the dark clouds of the storm, God's grace is still there.

When we don't think we can make it another day, God's grace is still there.

When we don't feel like we are enough, God's grace is still there.

We read this in the Letter to the Romans:

> God's law was given so that all people could see how sinful they were. But as people sinned more and more, God's wonderful *grace* became more abundant. So just as sin ruled over all people and brought them to death, now God's wonderful *grace* rules instead, giving us right standing with God and resulting in eternal life through Jesus Christ our Lord. (Rom. 5:20–21 NLT; italics mine)

Listen to Matthew West's song "Grace Wins Every Time." Christ's hand is still there upon you through the storm. Stop, pray, and ask for His grace; His unending mercy and favor shine through all the storms you are facing so that you can gain the strength to keep walking with the Lord. Let His grace help you today in your time of need.

DAY 25

Blessed

For he will be great in the sight of the Lord,
and shall drink neither wine nor strong drink. He
will also be filled with the Holy Spirit, even from
his mother's womb. (Luke 1:15 NIV)

During the last church service that I was pregnant, the preacher read this verse twice because he felt the verse had touched someone. The verse had spoken to my heart because I was pregnant with a son, and while I was pregnant, I had the overwhelming urge to drink alcohol because of my struggles. I never did drink, but I was planning to after I gave birth because I didn't want to harm the baby. In all honesty, being pregnant with my son made me draw closer to God for help instead of drowning my sorrows in a bottle of alcohol.

Now that my son is finally here for me to hold and cherish, I've turned to God's Word for the strength to not be consumed by alcohol. His word says, "Be sober, be vigilant [alert]; because your adversary the devil walks about like a roaring lion, seeking whom he may devour" (1 Pet. 5:8 NKJV).

The enemy hates us and wants to take our future, but God wants to give us a future. The devil will do everything in his power to keep us from experiencing anything good that Christ has to offer. He will do all that he can do to destroy us so that we do not have life in Christ. In the Gospel of John, we are told what the devil will do:

"The thief does not come except to steal, and to kill, and to destroy. I have come that they may have life, and that they may have it more abundantly" (John 10:10 NKJV).

The devil steals our joy that Christ has to offer. He wants to kill the plans that God has laid out for us before we were even formed in our mother's womb and destroy any hope of us obtaining a heavenly home.

The devil has been trying to take all my joy away and tempt me where he knows I am weak. But I know God has great plans for me, my son, and my family. My baby boy came amid a storm in our lives, facing the fresh diagnosis of type 1 diabetes in his sister. All excitement for him was laid aside during my pregnancy to help his sister, until he was born.

We have named our son Steven Asher, a blessed, shining light during the storm. Acts 6 speaks of the disciple with the Holy Spirit, Stephen, a man full of faith, full of God's grace and power. When all looked upon him, they saw the face of an angel. I know deep down my son is here for a reason—to let his light shine ever so bright in God's love. And because of this, I love singing the song "This Little Light of Mine" to Asher.

His light was already shining when I was pregnant, even when my excitement was lost. My son helped keep me from drinking alcohol and had me turning to God to find His grace during the storm. I boast of my weaknesses so that Christ's power may rest on me! I am reminded of His grace in the Word:

> But he said to me, "*My grace is sufficient for you, for my power is made perfect in weakness.*" Therefore I will boast all the more gladly about my weaknesses, so that Christ's power may rest on me. (2 Cor. 12:9; emphasis mine)

And since Asher has been born, he's been the happiest and most content child for us as we still battle the problems with Emma's diabetes. I truly do not understand how God works, but I do know His word is alive and powerful (Heb. 4:12). The enemy wants me to doubt Christ, but I want to testify and proclaim over my children that God has a mighty plan for them. He chose them for my husband and I, so I pray we raise them strong in Christ and are the vessels we need to be, to give them their future in God's love.

I write this testimony with the hopes of encouraging and strengthening your faith in Jesus Christ, our Savior. God really knew what He was doing when He blessed us with Asher, even when it felt like the worst timing ever. I could have allowed my situation to be the ruin of me, but instead I look at my son as a blessing.

If you're facing a storm today, think the timing is all wrong, and are finding yourself weak; take the time to lean on God's love and power by spending time in His word, and His rest will lie on you. Take a moment and ask God to search your heart for any weaknesses that you may have and hand them over to Him. Instead of focusing on your weaknesses, look for the blessings from the situation and focus on them. I pray that you can someday boast about your weaknesses and allow God's grace to be sufficient for you.

DAY 26

David and Goliath

Lately I have been wanting to take the time to read the story of David and Goliath because there is a story of them in my daughter's children's Bible. The story says that God blessed David and made him very brave. Since Emma's diagnosis of T1D, whenever she says she is scared to get her insulin shot or when we have to place a new Dexcom (continuous blood glucose monitor), I pray with her for God to bless her and make her brave like He did King David. So I made the time to read the story of David and Goliath in First Samuel 17 to fully comprehend his bravery.

The men of Israel were standing in fear of Goliath, a nine-foot-nine giant, for forty days! Every time they saw Goliath, they fled in fear. When David discovered the situation, his reaction was of faith in God. He proclaimed in verse 26, "Who is this uncircumcised Philistine that he should defy the armies of the Living God?" (1 Sam. 17:26 NIV).

David knew God was alive and more powerful than Goliath. While all the others fled in fear, David stood in his faith with God. We don't have to run in fear when we have God on our side! God is much more powerful than any past, present, and future fear that we encounter.

The Philistine Goliath came with his own power, but David came with God's power:

> David said to the Philistine, "You come against me with Sword and spear and javelin,

but I come against you in the name of the Lord Almighty, the God of the armies of Israel, whom you have defied... All those gathered here will know that it is not by sword or spear that the Lord saves; *for the battle is the Lord's* [italics mine], and he will give all of you into our hands." (1 Sam. 17:45, 47 NIV)

Ahh, isn't that bold proclamation so empowering! Because of his boldness, everyone else heard him testify of God's power, and they saw God's power work through David to defeat the giant Goliath. The motivation from David continues thousands of years later in me to not allow the giant of T1D to swallow me in fear but to allow God to strengthen me for the battle because the battle is His, not mine! My battle of constant lows and highs, carb counting, moodiness, exhaustion, middle-of-the-night snacks due to blood glucose (BG) drops, fear, insurance, cost of medical equipment and medicine, keeping a log for an eating schedule, always checking BG numbers to know when a snack or meal is needed, mental thoughts, baby brother, and all the other normal, typical, everyday life situations are not mine to fight alone! *The battle is the Lord's, and I boldly proclaim it like David. I will be bold in my faith so that others will see the mighty works of God during the battle.*

In the face of the Giant for Israel, the sight of Goliath was terrifying. Don't allow the sight of your battles to overcome you with fear like the army of Israel did. Don't run away from your battle and allow the enemy to win you over. Allow David's story to continue with you, thousands of years later. Step out in faith and boldly proclaim the power of God over your situation! I encourage you to hand over your battle to God and allow Him to take over, for the battle is His!

DAY 27

Time to Eat

With a newly diagnosed type 1 diabetic and a newborn son, all I feel like I accomplish every day are eating schedules. I am constantly looking at the clock and thinking, *Is it snack time? When did I dose for insulin last? How many carbs should Emma have now? When did Asher eat last? What time should I start lunch to have insulin and a snack before a nap?* The list can feel endless somedays!

On one particular day, I truly let worry consume me over an eating schedule. My type 1 diabetic was invited to a birthday party that was in between her mealtime schedule for insulin. I wanted my little girl to have a piece of cake so badly that I completely stressed over the timing for her to receive insulin for the cake and a meal. I almost didn't even go to the party, which would've hurt my daughter even more. I knew I couldn't keep carrying this burden on my own, so I went to God in prayer, asking for help with the anxiety of feeding Emma and Asher.

The next morning, I read my Bible devotion, and this passage leaped from the page and into my heart:

> Therefore I tell you, do not worry about
> your life, what you will eat or drink; or about
> your body, what you will wear. Is not life more
> than food, and the body more than clothes? Look
> at the birds of the air; they do not sow or reap or

store away in barns, and yet your heavenly Father feeds them. Are you not much more valuable than they? Can any one of you by worrying add a single hour to your life? (Matt. 6:25–27 NIV)

Wowza! Christ plainly says to not worry about what to eat or drink; *life is much more valuable than food!* And I feel like our lives revolve around food—eating, counting carbs, and dosing insulin. But life is so much more than this. Jesus values our lives so much that He references to how He feeds the birds. They don't have to sow, reap, or store away food like humans do; but our heavenly Father makes sure they are fed. So if He does this for the birds, how much more valuable are we? Worrying about these things will not add time to my life, and that is true! All this worrying I had been doing was taking precious time away from my family.

Jesus even repeats to not worry again because obviously He knows that we do:

So do not worry, saying, 'What shall we eat?' or 'What shall we wear?' For the pagans run after all these things, and your heavenly Father knows that you need them. But seek first his kingdom and his righteousness, and all these things will be given to you as well. Therefore do not worry about tomorrow, for tomorrow will worry about itself. Each day has enough trouble of its own. (Matt. 6:31–34 NIV)

Jesus already knows what we need so that we can live. Instead of worrying, He asks us to seek first the kingdom of God and His righteousness, and then all the things we need will be given to us. We don't not have to worry because the Lord will supply what we need.

If you continue reading into the next chapter, you'll read this:

Ask and it will be given to you; seek and you will find; knock and the door will be opened to you. For everyone who asks receives; the one who seeks finds; and to the one who knocks, the door will be opened. (Matt. 7:7–8 NIV)

I sought God through prayer again and thanked Him for considering me so valuable that I am more important than the food I had been worrying about. I asked Him to help me not worry about food or an eating schedule and to allow me to focus on what He wants me to see. Later that day, I discovered a no-carb gummy recipe from a friend. I went to buy the ingredients and found a no-carb Jell-O block mold building kit too! Then as I was checking out, in the midst of all the delicious holiday dessert magazines, there was a diabetic holiday food magazine! And as if that wasn't enough blessings, another friend invited me to join a keto and low-carb recipe group on Facebook! I stopped and praised God with tears for the small finds and the friends who helped along the way because if I would have continued to worry, I would have missed out on the blessings God laid out for me.

These Bible verses and blessings have reminded me to take this journey through the storm one day at a time. We don't have to worry about tomorrow; we can lay down our worries when we seek God first and ask Him for help often! Our life is quite more valuable to Him than the worries of this world. The next time you see a bird flying by or singing a lovely song, remember that if God takes care of them so that they don't have to worry, He will do even more for you.

DAY 28

Live in the Moment

Quite often I struggle with living in the moment. I read countless articles about living in the present, to not live in the past and to not live in the future. I hear people say often to soak the moments up with your kids now because they grow up too fast. It's all true, and when I read those articles or hear people's advice, I briefly live in the moment until something comes up. My son needs food, my daughter needs a snack, laundry needs washed, bottles need made, tempers need dealt with—all these things distract me from living in the moment.

As I was actually enjoying a moment of quiet while washing bottles, I started thinking that the days aren't meant to be merely survived but to be fully lived. I took a deep breath and prayed for help to live fully each day, and the Bible verse from John 10:10 came to my mind: "The thief does not come except to steal, and to kill, and to destroy. I have come that they may have life, and that they may have it more abundantly" (John 10:10 NKJV).

Abundantly—a life lived fully where the enemy doesn't steal, kill, and destroy. I kept thinking about the word *abundantly*. How do I get this fullness in life? I reflected back to the Bible verse and read it again. I can have this full, abundant life because Jesus Christ came to this earth for us to live fully with Him so that the enemy doesn't steal our lives away.

I breathed deep again. *Live fully in the moment. One breath, one step, one word of God at a time.* I only needed one Bible verse to help me remember God's fullness and help me come back to the moment—one verse to help me not dwell on the million things that need done but the full life that is happening right there in front of me, right now.

I took a sip of my coffee and read the words on the cup. *Saved by grace.* I thought upon the word *grace* and connected the word with John 10:10. By Christ's grace, He was able to give us a life full of abundance by dying on the cross for our sins. This beautiful act of love saves us from the enemy trying to steal and destroy our lives! The word *grace* brought my mind to part of another verse, "My Grace is sufficient for you." I looked up the Bible verse and read the whole passage:

> But he said to me, "My grace is sufficient for you, for my power is made perfect in weakness." Therefore I will boast all the more gladly about my weaknesses, so that Christ's power may rest on me. (2 Cor. 12:9 NIV)

Christ's grace is sufficient (is enough) for us when we are weak with the devil's temptations to steal us from our moments. The devil steals our joy, fills us with doubts, destroys our self-control, and tempts us to focus on anything possible that will fill us with anxiety. But the good news is that Christ's power rests on us in our weaknesses so that we can live that abundant, full life!

Momma, if you will, pause with me for a moment. Take a deep breath and pray to live fully in each moment. Pray for God's strength when you are weak and falling away from the life-filled moments. May God's grace be sufficient for you and me.

DAY 29

Peace, Be Still

On the same day, when evening had come, He said to them, *"Let us cross over to the other side."* Now when they had left the multitude, they took Him along in the boat as He was. And other little boats were also with Him. And a great windstorm arose, and the waves beat into the boat, so that it was already filling. But He was in the stern, asleep on a pillow. And they awoke Him and said to Him, "Teacher, do You not care that we are perishing?" Then He arose and rebuked the wind, and said to the sea, *"Peace, be still!"* And the wind ceased and there was a *great calm.* But He said to them, *"Why are you so fearful? How is it that you have no faith?"* And they feared exceedingly, and said to one another, "Who can this be, that even the wind and the sea obey Him?"
—Mark 4:35–41 NKJV; italics mine

I read these verses and fall in love with the goodness of Christ even more. Jesus and His disciples were in a boat in the sea, and a great windstorm arose. This was a storm so furious that waves were sweeping over the boat. I am sure the boat was swaying back and forth and the screeching wind swallowed their hearts with fear! Yet Jesus was sleeping peacefully through the raging storm on a pillow. The disciples were so scared of the storm killing them that they sought Jesus for help, woke Him up, and stated their fears. Jesus arose and said three simple words, *"Peace, be still."* With the short utterance from

His lips, the winds ceased, and there was a great calm—a complete quiet and peace in the middle of the storm. Jesus then questioned the disciples and asked why they were so fearful. Why did they let fear overcome their faith in Christ? They feared because the disciples did not have enough faith in Christ to remain in peace during the storm.

The men were so amazed that they proclaimed in astonishment that Christ controlled the storm and couldn't believe the miracle before their eyes. They were in complete shock that Jesus Christ could control the essence of the storm! If they would have had more faith in Christ's power, then they would not have been in such amazement when He stopped the storm before their eyes. They would have already had enough trust in Him to settle their fears.

Now read this story and place yourself in the disciple's shoes. How often do we allow fear to grip our souls instead of placing our faith in Jesus Christ? Jesus was showing by example that we can sleep like Him when the winds of our storms rage in our lives. With faith in Christ's power and love for us, He can bring upon us a great calm as we face the waves and wind in our storm. We do not have to live in fear of the storm surrounding us because Christ wants us to not be afraid and have faith in Him. He has the power to rebuke the essence of our storm so that we can rest peacefully. The fears that rage inside of you, the storms that rise up around you—Jesus Christ can silence them with just an utterance from His lips, "*Peace, be still!*"

Remember, Christ leaves us a peace of mind that the world cannot give so that our hearts won't be troubled or afraid (John 14:27). We are more than conquerors through Christ because He has *overcome* the world! The Gospel of John reminds us, "These things I have spoken to you, that in Me you may have peace. In the world you will have tribulation; but be of good cheer, I have overcome the world" (John 16:33 NKJV).

Oh, I just love this verse! The hope in the words sends a tingling sensation of joy right into my heart. In all the waves and winds during our tribulation, we can find joy because Jesus has overcome the world! Even more, not only did Christ overcome the world, but He did so for us so that He can now live in us and help us overcome the world too! First John 4:4 tells us, "You are of God, little children, and have overcome them, because He who is in you is greater than he who is in the world" (1 John 4:4 NKJV).

Christ, God's Son who came to this earth to die for our sins, now lives in us. He is greater than the tribulations we face. He is greater than the storm that swallows us up and drowns us in sorrows. He lives in us so that we can conquer the world with Him. We cannot survive the storm alone, and Christ knows that. He resides in us to speak over our storm, "*Peace, be still!*" so that we can have His great calm to walk through the storm with faith instead of fear.

Momma, I encourage you to practice applying this faith in your life by taking a deep breath and speaking the words "Peace, be still!" when fears and anxieties rise in your heart. Make the effort to switch your mind to the peaceful words of the Bible before you react in fear. The Lord's great calm comes with practice and by trusting in Him!

DAY 30

Character Builder

Not only so, but we also glory in our sufferings, because we know that suffering produces perseverance; perseverance, character; and character, hope. And hope does not put us to shame, because God's love has been poured out into our hearts through the Holy Spirit, who has been given to us.
—Rom. 5:3–5 NIV

One evening, I really lost my cool. My daughter was having a temper tantrum, and my son was very fussy. Instead of walking away, I matched my daughter's temper and screamed back at her, even spanking her harder than I should have. Afterward, I felt completely horrible for the way I reacted and was heavy with guilt. (Sadly, this hadn't been the only time I lost my cool and made mistakes.) I am not perfect, and thankfully, God still loves me. That evening, I prayed with Emma for forgiveness and asked God to help me be better from this mistake. My sweet, precious, type 1 diabetic girl forgave me and reminded me to take deep breaths.

The next morning, shortly after Emma woke up, she wanted to dress herself for the first time. She did great until she couldn't get her sweatshirt on and became very upset. I was patient and encouraged her through the struggle, which led her to calm back down. Afterward, I started to think about this moment and the bad moment I had the previous night. The night before, I failed; and this morning, God's grace helped me. I didn't give up but persevered in this season of T1D, temper tantrums, newborn needs, and being home with them to adjust to it all. I had prayed to be with my babies in this season and am thankful for it, but I had not entered this season gracefully. But isn't that why we go through different seasons?

Let's reflect on Romans 5:3–5. We go through these things to build our perseverance (patience) and character. I am by far not perfect in this new season, but I can persevere with God to build my character in Him, and I can have God's hope through it all. All the effort and work to build our patience and character will not be done in vain. And though we will make mistakes, we don't have to stay in the shame of them because we have God's hope of love being poured into our hearts. He will forgive us, and His love will encourage us to persevere! Take this passage from the Epistle of James:

> My brethren, count it *all joy* when you fall into various trials, *knowing* that the testing of your faith produces patience. But let patience have its perfect work, that you may be perfect and complete, lacking nothing. (James 1:2–4 NKJV; emphasis mine)

Say what? We are to consider it *all joy* when we face trials? Yes! And the reason is because Jesus is doing a good work in us (Phil. 1:6)! Through the trial, we will become better in our character and patience, reflecting God's light! The enemy knows what our weaknesses are and tries even harder to break us with that weakness, but the trial produces patience in us and increases our hope and faith in the Lord's salvation. The enemy thinks he is winning, but when we go forward with Jesus, he won't win! I love the way Grace School of Theology, in partnership with El Centro Network, worded their input on this verse in their devotional *Golden Repair:*

> James is telling us to take a step back and see the Lord in the middle of the trial and to have all joy. Not a little joy or some joy, but all

joy. Literally total joy, joy that is not tainted by depression or self-pity. Why? Because they can see Christ in the middle of the trial. Also, James uses the word knowing. In the Greek this is a word that translates to know by experience. So, how do we respond to trials? With joy, because we know and have experienced Christ in the midst of our trials.

Now, all this character building truly won't go in vain. We have the capability to better ourselves and help guide others when we establish ourselves in the Lord. My daughter has a ginormous battle to face the rest of her life with her autoimmune disease. She can either resort to anger over the bad card that she's been dealt or she can build her perseverance and character because of the trial. While I have the hope to be a better person and closer to God through this storm, I can also model this behavior for my children as they face their own obstacles in life.

This season will probably be a long journey, but I can find joy facing this trial because of the outcome that will come forth from it. "To everything there is a season, a time for every purpose under Heaven," Ecclesiastes 3:1 (NKJV) reminds us.

I am in a season of suffering, but I am finding joy through the process. This season is giving me an opportunity for growth in my character as I raise my littles. I am thankful for this season, for the opportunity to be better, and to watch my children grow. I am thankful that I will not be put to shame through my mistakes, but I can place my hope in God and have His love.

As you go through your season of suffering, reflect on your weaknesses and seek the Lord to help you build your character and perseverance. Don't stay in the shame of your mistakes but ask for forgiveness and make the effort to be who God wants you to be through this trial. Allow God's hope to pour into your heart and remind yourself daily, if you have to, that this trial will not go in vain.

We don't go through a trial just to stay the same, but God can use the trial to work on you and change you for the better. We go through a trial because there's a greater purpose at the end of it. We don't know what will happen at the end of the trial, but we can have faith that there will be a beautiful outcome from it. Our suffering allows us to grow in our character to become who God has always intended for us to be.

DAY 31

Begging for Mercy

Now they came to Jericho. As He went out of Jericho with
His disciples and a great multitude, blind Bartimaeus, the
son of Timaeus, sat by the road begging. And when he
heard that it was Jesus of Nazareth, he began to cry out
and say, "Jesus, Son of David, have mercy on me!"
Then many warned him to be quiet; but he cried out
all the more, "Son of David, have mercy on me!"
So Jesus stood still and commanded him to be called.
Then they called the blind man, saying to him,
"Be of good cheer. Rise, He is calling you."
And throwing aside his garment, he rose and came to Jesus.
So Jesus answered and said to him, "*What
do you want Me to do for you?*"
The blind man said to Him, "Rabboni,
that I may receive my sight."
Then Jesus said to him, "*Go your way; your faith
has made you well.*" And immediately he received
his sight and followed Jesus on the road.
—Mark 10:46–52 NKJV; italics mine

B artimaeus was a beggar and was in his lowest state, begging, as
Jesus and a great multitude was passing by. When the beggar
heard that Jesus of Nazareth was passing by, he cried out to Him, say-

ing, "Jesus, Son of David, have mercy on me!" (v 47). This lowly person whom many people often reject was warned to be quiet. People saw Jesus as such a great wonder that they didn't want this lowly beggar bothering Him. They may have even thought that the beggar was going to ask for money! Yet they forgot that Jesus didn't come to serve the righteous, but He came to serve the lowly who needed Him and His salvation. Jesus didn't come to pick and choose whom to save; He came to save us all.

Knowing that Jesus was walking by brought out the beggar's greatest desire, his want for sight. Just knowing that Jesus was walking by was enough to convict his heart to not stay a beggar but to become a person with sight. I see this as more than just having sight to see everything before him. No, I see this as Bartimaeus begging Jesus for mercy, for His compassion and forgiveness. He wanted his eyes opened to Christ's goodness, His mercy, and His love. He wanted to see Jesus's way and not the way he had been living to make him in the lowly state he had become. It had probably taken him years to become so low, to beg for others to support his sinful lifestyle, and it only took one moment for Jesus to pass by for the sinner's heart to be convicted.

As the crowd tried to quiet the beggar, he cried out all the more for Jesus to have mercy on him. Even though the people were bringing him down, trying to stop his newfound faith, the beggar longed for that healing. He longed to be well, and he didn't want the opportunity to pass him by. This beggar had great faith in Jesus and didn't want to live a worldly life anymore. He didn't want a temporary fix anymore with quick cash, which could've led to drunkenness. No. He wanted an eternal fix that Jesus offered—the hope that Christ gives out abundantly.

Reflecting on the beggar's actions, I started to question my own actions. How often do I stay in my lowly state and let Christ's goodness pass me by? How often do I keep my sight on my woes and my worries instead of the joy of Christ? How often do I focus on the things that will exhaust me instead of the blessings right here before me? How often do I even dread the tiring lies of the enemy instead of being filled to the point of overflowing with Christ's love and mercy?

I so often choose to be blind to Christ's love and mercy all around me that I miss Jesus walking by. Do I beg for others to fix my problems like the blind man? Do I become mad when things don't go my way? Yes, I answer yes and plead guilty. And now here Jesus is, convicting my heart as I pacify a fussy four-month-old on my lap. He is reminding me yet again to not focus on the problems around me but to open my eyes to see His mercy before me, to long and beg for His presence in my everyday moments of life.

Seeing Christ's mercy is a practice and a desire to come out of the darkness of negative thoughts and to stop begging for perfectness from others when we aren't perfect ourselves. I reread the passage of the blind man again. After Bartimaeus cried for mercy more than once, Jesus stood still (v 49). He took the time to stop for the sinner who wanted His mercy, His unfailing love. Jesus called for His lost sheep and the multitude saw Jesus's mercy. They changed their attitudes and encouraged the man to "be of good cheer. Rise, He is calling you." Rise. Stand up to Jesus's calling. Desire His mercy. He will stand still for you to meet Him at His feet.

Just imagine all the suffering you've faced, and through it all you hear Jesus gently speak to you, *"Rise. I am calling you,"* calling you for a deeper and better life with Him—a life so good that you throw off your old garment of sin and come running to Him (v 50).

Now take a moment and read Colossians 3:5–14. Paul asks us to "throw off the old garment" by putting to death our earthly nature—sexual immorality, impurity, lust, evil desires, and greed, which is idolatry. He says you used to walk in these ways, in the life you once lived. But now you must also rid yourselves of all things such as anger, rage, malice, slander, and filthy language from your lips. We must take off our old selves with these sinful practices and put on the new self, "the new garment," which is being renewed in knowledge in the image of its Creator. "A new garment" clothed with compassion, kindness, humility, gentleness, and patience—to forgive as the Lord forgives us. And over all these virtues, put on love, which binds them all together in perfect unity. Christ's mercy (compassion and forgiveness) meets us in the middle as we put to death our old ways.

As the beggar throws off his old ways, Christ asks, "What do you want Me to do for you?" and the blind man said, "Rabboni, that I may receive my sight" (v 51)—not a sight to continue seeing the old ways of sin but the renewed sight of living with Christ, a sight with seeing His love and being His love. And Jesus replied, "Go your way; your faith has made you well," and immediately he received his sight and followed Jesus on the road (v 52).

The convicted heart of the beggar had faith in Jesus's mercy. His faith made him well, which left his old ways behind and allowed Him to see Christ's mercy, to feel and know His unfailing love. His was a faith so rich that he continued to follow Jesus afterward because the new life in Him was so much better than his old life of sin.

Your faith in Christ allows you to put to death your old nature and rid yourself of the things that hinder you to know Christ. Your faith allows you to be renewed and live well—not live in anger, not live in rage, but to live well in love and the fruits of the spirit. And here Christ is, reaching out for a sinner like me, a beggar begging for mercy, taking me deeper into His love and making me well through my faith in Him. He came for all, even me. I pray my convicted heart will encourage you to throw off your old garment of sin and replace it with a sight fixed on Jesus and His unfailing mercy. Hear the call of Christ to rise and choose to go into a journey deeper with Him.

DAY 32

How Long, Lord?

How long, Lord? Will you forget me forever?
How long will you hide your face from me?
How long must I wrestle with my thoughts
and day after day have sorrow in my heart?
How long will my enemy triumph over me?
—Ps. 13:1–2 NIV

David said in several verses, "How long?" and questioned God about how much longer should he suffer, even saying the enemy would overcome him if He did not give light to his eyes and answer (Ps. 13:3–4). Even though David questioned God and was hurting, he continued to say to the Lord,

But I trust in your unfailing love;
my heart rejoices in your salvation.
I will sing the Lord's praise,
for He has been good to me. (Ps. 13:5–6 NIV)

David finished his prayer with trust in God's unfailing love and rejoiced in the Lord's salvation. According to Dictionary.com, *salvation* is the "deliverance from harm, ruin, or loss," deliverance from sin brought by faith in Christ. The Lord's salvation delivers us from the harm of sin, from hell, and that is definitely something worth rejoicing in! Even though he was still suffering in his storm of troubles, he praised with worship to God and reflected on the good God had already done in his life.

There are several stories in the Bible where people had to go through numerous situations of suffering. While they were going through the trial, they kept their faith in the Lord and worshipped in the waiting. David sang praises to the Lord during his suffering. Paul and Silas were beaten and thrown into prison, and while they were in prison, they chose to pray and sing hymns to God (Acts 16:25). God used them in prison to save souls because their praise was heard by other prisoners! Not only did these courageous men worship during pain, but Jesus even sang hymns during his suffering! When Jesus had taken His last drink from the fruit of the vine that He was ever going to drink here on earth, He knew death was knocking at His door. So He choose to worship amid the pain instead of giving into the heartache.

We read this in the Gospel of Mark:

> *Truly I tell you, I will not drink again from the fruit of the vine until that day when I drink it new in the kingdom of God.*
> When they had sung a hymn, they went out to the Mount of Olives. (Mark 14:25–26 NIV; emphasis mine)

Imagine the sorrow gripping at His heart! However, He still chose to worship the Lord. David, Paul, Silas, and Christ all knew of the healing power of worship amid pain and sorrow. And during the praise, they were humbled. David acknowledges that God is greater, even though he questioned the Lord's timing. With Jesus, He went to the garden of Gethsemane to pray soon after His worship. Jesus knew the cruel death He was about to face and hoped that He didn't have to drink the cup of death upon the cross. He prayed, "Abba, Father, *all things are possible for You*. Take this cup away from Me; nevertheless, not what I will, but what You will" (Mark 14:36 NKJV).

God can truly do anything! But what an act of humility for Christ to do God's will even though He was almost to the point of death just from grief (v 34). Christ didn't want to suffer, just as much as the others did not want to suffer anymore.

I can remember so clearly the deep anguish I felt the day when my daughter was diagnosed with type 1 diabetes. Through the whirlwind of emotions and the diagnosis that instantly changed our lives in one day, I remembered the song "Even If" by MercyMe and Bart Millard's testimony of his type 1 diabetic son.

I had to take a breather and step outside by myself for a moment. The day was as warm and beautiful as could be, but my world felt like dark clouds of lightning were striking me down. I found a memorial garden and sat on a bench that overlooked the river. In this moment, I decided to listen to the song "Even If" and lift some kind of praise from my lips. As I was crying the words to the song, I felt a hug of comfort pour over me. No one was beside me on the bench, but I could feel the Lord's presence holding me tight, letting me know I wasn't going to walk this storm alone.

Since that day, there have been several moments where I have humbled myself to my knees and cried by the beside to the Lord. The moment that Christ experienced comes to my mind so often as I kneel, crying out to the Lord for strength for my daughter and me. I often cry to the Lord in prayer with fervent tears, telling God of my hurt. I practically beg the Lord to take this cup away from us, to let the suffering stop. And as I pray Christ's prayer, I humble myself and say, "Not my will but Your will, Lord."

One evening during my heart-wrenched praying, the Lord reminded me that He was no stranger to the pain that I feel. He watched His own son suffer too. He watched and heard His son cry out in prayer with deeper anguish than mine, but Christ had to suffer in order to save many lives. In our own families' journey, I believe we will have to suffer too because many lives will be saved through the pain. And to help, God sent an angel to strengthen Christ as He suffered (Luke 22:43), which reminds me of the comfort I felt the day I uttered praise from my lips after Emma's diagnosis.

A sermon also comes to my mind by our pastor, Damon Davis. I can hear his preaching now resonating in boldness:

> Situations will arise and worry will fill your mind. The enemy will do all that he can to hinder you from God's grace. When you're caught in the storm and doubts/worries fill your mind, turn your thoughts into worship. Turn on music and start singing praises to God. Start praying to God and praising Him for all the good He has done and all that He is going to do. Start focusing on the good and make the devil flee.

The Epistle of James tells us what we must do in our suffering: "Submit yourselves, then, to God. Resist the devil, and he will flee from you" (James 4:7 NIV). The devil wants you to be consumed and turn from God, but choose to resist the devil and he will be the one fleeing, not you! If you continue to read in James, we read, "Humble yourselves before the Lord, and he will lift you up" (James 4:10 NIV).

So like David, I wonder how long my mind will suffer negative thoughts? How long will I suffer from the lies of the enemy? How long will the diabetic journey last? How long will obstacles arise as I parent two children? But my questions aren't getting me anywhere! I am allowing the enemy to win me over when I allow these negative thoughts and questions to sink in. Like David, I can worship and reflect on the good instead of the things that cause me suffering. And like Christ, Paul, and Silas, I can keep worshiping and praying in the waiting of the diabetic and parenting journey, submitting and humbling myself to the Lord's plan for my life.

Do you have suffering that causes you to ask "How long?" Maybe it's how long will these tempers last or how long will this rebellion last? The journey may be short or it may last a whole lifetime. However long the journey may be, choose to let your praises and worship be lifted up to the Lord in the middle of the pain. According to Katherine Wolf from her book *Suffer Strong*, she states, "Worship in its purest form doesn't happen when everything comes perfectly together; it's most powerful when everything is falling apart." So today, choose to worship in the middle of the hurt. You never know just how many lives are going to be saved through your suffering and your worship, just like Paul and Silas! And as you cry in worship remember this:

> Those who sow with tears
> will reap with songs of joy.
> Those who go out weeping,
> carrying seed to sow,
> will return with songs of joy,
> carrying sheaves [the harvest] with them. (Ps. 126:5–6 NIV)

As you go through your journey with the Lord, remember all the tears that you are shedding will one day be reaped up into a beautiful harvest with songs of joy. For now, the songs will be sung with tears and pain, but one day, the songs will be sung with joy because of the glorious harvest you will reap from the pain that you have sown.

DAY 33

Thank You, Lord

Praise the Lord.
Give thanks to the Lord, for He is good;
his love endures forever.
—Ps. 106:1 NIV

I've been reading the book *One Thousand Gifts* by Ann Voskamp and discovering a whole new joy in life by thankfulness. Her journey has been an enriching read that has truly helped me find a deeper love in Christ through thankfulness as I parent my children and search God's heart. I must give honor where honor is due because without her guidance—as well as the guidance, encouragement, love, and prayers of many others—my heart could not grasp the thankfulness and fullness of God's love that I have come to know through the journey of searching for Him.

In Psalms, David praised and thanked the Lord so many times for all the good He had shown Him. David was a man after God's own heart, and He knew the beauty in gratitude. David started many Psalms with thankfulness, including Psalms 106:1, 107:1, 118:1, and 136:1, all from different circumstances. Along with giving thanks, David recognized God's love, His mercy, and how His love lasts forever—a love that outlives our lives and goes on and on, a love that endures with our children and with their children.

This love I've come to take root in, I find in the heartache. One morning, my daughter hit a high blood sugar of 387, with a reading on her continuous blood glucose monitor of a steady increase. I googled the symptoms of high blood sugar to remind me of the way she was feeling right then. She felt fatigued, thirsty, and possible blurred vision with a headache. My heart hurt. I proceeded to google "low blood sugar symptoms" to remind me of more pain, to remind me she feels confusion, dizziness, shakiness, irritability, fatigue, and blurred vision when her blood sugar goes low.

I looked at my precious daughter as she played a game on her iPad, and I told her with a smile that I loved her. She looked up, smiled back, and said, "I love you too, Mommy." And while I looked at my beloved girl, imagining the way she was feeling right then, not complaining, realizing she will feel these symptoms the rest of her life, a song of comfort played on Pandora. The song reminded me to sleep and rest in the storm. The song was by Unspoken and had given me comfort many times before, which reminded me yet again that God has it *all* under His control. I looked at my son, and he simply smiled at me with not a worry in the world.

Every day diabetes is a reminder that each day is a gift of life. Quickly it could go out of control, and Emma's life could slip away. But each day is a gift of peace and love from Christ. Each day I find thanks and remember she is still here with me. Even if diabetes wasn't here, each day is still a gift. We don't know what tomorrow or the day holds. Diabetes just makes me more aware that life is happening right now: Emma is still here giving me her innocent smile of love through the icky symptoms, and my son is here laughing in the middle of it all.

I often thank the Lord for their smiles and realize *love is all around us*. God is everywhere, sinking deep into my heart, singing my soul into His comfort, His peace. My trust in Him keeps me in peace with the crazy highs and lows of everyday life. His love helps me not worry about tomorrow because He has given me the gift of today, with joy in the middle of the pain. It's all around me; I just have to open my eyes to His love and His blessings and allow myself to give thanks for it all.

I embraced Emma in my arms and imagined me feeling her symptoms, the glucose that is lost in her body and cannot enter her cells to nourish them because her insulin-producing beta cells are killed by her own cells! Without insulin, her cells cannot open up to allow the glucose in. Her own body attacked itself, confused, and now one small detail that can't function properly sends her body into possible death every day. The body so perfectly knitted together by God has lost one of His fine details and can't function without His intricate design. But Jesus—He breathes life into the death of the simple life we once knew. He breathes life into heartbreak, new hope into what has been lost. His promises are greater than I ever imagined.

My sweet, sweet girl shines bright amid the death that lingers in her body because the God of all hope is alive in her, fighting her battle for her. And this is love: new life in what is dead and new life in the hope of a bright life because she is still here to proclaim hope. This is a new love that we have never known because of the old life that was laid to rest and the new life in Christ in which He has clothed us and lives in us—the life that lives in my daughter, in my son, in all of us. I lay aside the anger, I lay aside the hurt, and I give thanks in the pain.

Emma could be dead, but she's not. Each day is a gift with her, with Asher, with my husband, and with me alive. Let us love while we can. We are not promised tomorrow. Let us hope while we can and bring life from the death. Let's breathe life into our children so that they can shine bright among the dark in the world. We are able to smile in the storm because Christ's love is alive. I've been blessed to see this deeper love of Christ because of the death in my daughter's pancreas, the love that all started from her birth. I can let the fears and hardships of every day be laid to rest because of Christ's peace that carries me through.

I pray often to see the blessings while I hurt, the blessings that I can give thanks for. My continuous thanks in all circumstances. The circumstances that should bring death but is brought to life by Christ. The Word reminds us to "rejoice always, pray continually, give thanks in all circumstances; for this is God's will for you in Christ Jesus" (1 Thess. 5:16–18 NIV)

This journey has brought about a new life of love in Christ through gratitude. Finding the blessings in all the moments, the hard ones and the good ones, lifts my heart to a new level of joy and a deeper love in Christ. I pray, Momma, that you may find the blessings to give thanks for and continue to find them each and every day. I encourage you to practice searching for things to be thankful for during good moments and during bad moments. The more you practice finding the good, the easier you will see the good in all situations of your life. You are loved, Momma, and that is a wonderful thing to be thankful for!

DAY 34

Picture-Worthy Moment

The window in my kitchen has a front-row view to the coal train that passes by multiple times every day. A mile down the road, there is a coal-loading station; and the train will stop in front of the house, load coal, and then haul the coal away. Every day I see the trains, hear their familiar rumble, and see the artwork on the sides of the coal cars. I have become so used to the train that I can hear the rumble from far away and know the train is coming.

One spring morning, I noticed from my kitchen window two men parked at the end of my driveway. I was very curious why these men were parked there and decided to watch them. Both men got out of the car and opened the trunk to pull out a camera for each of them. They then proceeded to change the lens on their cameras and adjust the settings. As they did so, I prayed for the beauty they were going to capture in their lens and that others would be blessed by what they saw. When they finished adjusting their cameras, they aimed their viewpoint down the railroad tracks, of which I imagined they were seeing deer. Then I heard the familiar rumble, and I smiled. They were captivated by the coal train getting ready to pass by—the train that I had become familiar with and forgotten how captivating its beauty was. Little did I know that I had actually prayed for myself to be blessed by what they saw.

I redirected my thoughts and came back to the moment I was in before I was intrigued by the photographers. I was in the middle of calculating the amount of insulin my daughter needed for her breakfast. Quickly, a memory flashed through my mind from a previous day. A coal car that stopped closely by my kitchen window had painted on the side "God loves you." That moment and that memory were happening for a reason. My heart and mind were quieted as I stared at my daughter's insulin pens in my hands. I proceeded to ask God, "What are you trying to lay on my heart right now?"

I connected the beauty of the train with my life. The blessings that I had become used to were the blessings with which He continuously blessed me, day in and day out. I had become used to the blessings and forgot their goodness. Oh my! I immediately asked the Lord, "Forgive me, Lord, for being stuck in the habit, the sight of the ugly. For being stuck in my selfishness and forsaking you, when you never forsook me. Forgive me for forsaking the beauty of my children, the gifts you placed before me. Forgive me, Lord, for becoming *used to* and expectant of your familiar, everyday blessings. Forgive me for forgetting the beauty of what others see as beautiful, I take for granted!" I even realized that the moments where my daughter is strong with the Lord's strength, when she receives her shots, I was taking for granted!

I then remembered how I had taken for granted our simple life with eating whatever we wanted, when we wanted. And now, that blessing is gone due to type 1 diabetes. Even worse, I was starting to become used to the blessings again with our new lifestyle that is complicated by an autoimmune disease. I was taking for granted the blessing of Emma's good health as she plays. Before her diagnosis, she was so sick with high blood sugar that I had to carry her everywhere because of her exhaustion. We barely admitted her into the hospital in time because they gave her a week to live if we hadn't brought her in when we did. More so, I had just woken up that morning extremely tired from staying up late and feeding my son in the middle of the night. I woke up wanting a lazy day, wishing I could sleep instead of being my fullest for the kids.

The Lord humbled me with the picture-worthy moment that always passes by my kitchen window. I prayed again, "Oh Lord, in this T1D life now, in the moments my daughter is strong with your strength, may I never forget that You were the one to bless her with this strength. May I never forsake what you have given me and allow it to become a *used-to* blessing where I expect more from you. I want the sight to see the goodness each and every day—to not take for granted the little but to swell with gratitude from the beauty that God gifts to us. May I see and remember the picture-worthy moments as I am with my children."

This passage from the Gospel of Matthew came to my memory as I prayed:

"For to everyone who has [and values his blessings and gifts from God, and has used them wisely], more will be given, and [he will be richly supplied so that] he will have an abundance; but from the one who does not have [because he has ignored or disregarded his blessings and gifts from God], even what he does have will be taken away. (Matt. 25:29 AMP)

I don't want to disregard and ignore my blessings anymore because I don't want them taken away! I want to value these blessings, these gifts from God, and use them wisely.

My selfishness of taking for granted God's blessings led me to recall the Israelites and their wondering in the wilderness for forty years. In Exodus 14:31, Israel saw the great work from the Lord and feared Him. They sang to the Lord, praising Him for bringing them out of Egypt (Exod. 15:1–2). But soon in the next verses and chapters, they murmured against Moses several times, saying to him, "You have brought us out into this desert to starve this entire assembly to death" or questioned, "What shall we drink?" They even threatened to stone Moses to death to get what they wanted!

The Israelites continuously received blessings but forgot about them all. They expected more instead of staying grateful and humble. They became ungrateful for what they had been given and became *used to* the blessings like me. Even though they saw God work through

Moses to split the sea and save them from the Egyptians, they quickly forgot. They continuously complained and kept losing faith in God.

I confess, I had seen God restore life back into my daughter and quickly forgot this blessing. Even the goodness of the everyday life moments, I had taken for granted and instead complained about. God knows I am human and my flesh is weak. I want to accept the beauty of what God has gifted me with and quit being ungrateful, always expecting more. The Lord gives me what I need, when I need it, as is said in the Word: "And my God will meet all your needs according to the riches of his glory in Christ Jesus" (Phil. 4:19 NIV).

Are there picture-worthy moments in your life that you have become *used to* and taken for granted like me? We are all human and tend to forget these blessings when times are hard, but we can redirect our minds to Christ's goodness. Take a moment like I did and ask God to forgive you for taking for granted His beautiful blessings. Pray that He will open your eyes to see the goodness each and every day—to not take for granted the little but to swell with gratitude from the beauty that God gifts to you. May you see and remember the picture-worthy moments each day you are with your children.

DAY 35

Refined

But He knows the way that I take;
When He has tested me,
I shall come forth as gold.
—Job 23:10 NKJV

According to the gold-refining company Pease and Curren, the most accurate method of refining gold is the fire method, further expounding,

> Refining gold is very involved and requires many steps. The process is *worth the time and effort* it takes because it has been proven to be twenty times more accurate than any other method. Even though it is the most used process for gold; it can be time-consuming. Raw gold that is found in the Earth is *first crushed* to separate the gold from the surrounding elements. The gold is then *beaten and melted* by a fire to separate the gold from the elements that contaminate it. (Pease and Curren website; italics mine)

Did you notice the words that are emphasized? Refining gold with the fire method is worth the time and effort because of its accuracy. Gold is crushed, beaten, and melted. Many steps are required, but the process is worth the beauty in the end. These words and steps by Pease and Curren are the methods to which Job is referring. This method that Job suggests that God uses to test us does not sound very pleasing, does it? To be crushed, beaten, and then melted sounds quite severe! Job realizes there is a reason behind the harsh ways of refining though. This is the most accurate process for gold to become pure. So refining us is the most accurate way to rid ourselves of the impurities that keep us from having a pure, genuine faith in God.

Peter brings to our attention the refining process too:

> In all this you greatly rejoice, though now for a little while you may have had to suffer grief in all kinds of trials. These have come so that the proven genuineness of your faith—of greater worth than gold, which perishes even though refined by fire—may result in praise, glory and honor when Jesus Christ is revealed. Though you have not seen him, you love him; and even though you do not see him now, you believe in him and are filled with an inexpressible and glorious joy, for you are receiving the end result of your faith, the salvation of your souls. (1 Pet. 1:6–9 NIV)

Gold perishes and doesn't last in the pure state forever, even though it is refined to become pure. Our faith is being refined and tested. We are crushed, beaten, and burned by our trials and by our sufferings. These trials come to rid us of the elements that make us dirty. They come to refine us so that our faith will be pure. Gold is refined by fire to become pure, unhindered by other elements. Our faith is refined by trials to become pure from sin and our fleshly nature—so pure, we can rejoice because the result will be of praise, glory, and honor when Jesus Christ is revealed! Our faith is worth more than gold. Refining gold is a hard and complicated process, so is refining our faith. *All kinds of trials* have to happen in order to have the proven genuineness of our faith, which is of greater worth than gold!

God's inexpressible and glorious joy will meet us in the trial. The joy of the Lord is different from just being happy because happiness depends on what happens to us. The Lord's joy is rooted down into His heart and His love by having Jesus Christ in our lives. Christ's grace is already poured on us through His death, and we can have hope that beauty will come from this trial. The trial is testing and refining our faith, but our faith will come forth with greater worth than gold if we do not give up! We are receiving the end result of our faith—the salvation of our souls.

Jesus led a life by example so that He could empathize with our suffering. At the beginning of Christ's ministry, after He was baptized, the Gospel of Luke describes how He was led by the Spirit into the wilderness: "Then Jesus, being filled with the Holy Spirit, returned from the Jordan and was led by the Spirit into the wilderness, being tempted for forty days by the devil" (Luke 4:1–2 NKJV).

By Christ being led by the Spirit into the wilderness, we see that God allows temptation into our lives so that our faith can be strengthened. As you continue to read, Jesus is weak with hunger but still resisted the temptation of the devil with the word of God. When the temptation ended, we read, "Then Jesus returned in the power of the Spirit to Galilee, and news of Him went out through all the surrounding region" (Luke 4:14 NKJV).

Jesus returned from the testing of temptation by the devil with the power of the Spirit! We become stronger when we face temptations and resist them with God on our side!

All the trials that I have faced, I have come to desire to lay my impurities aside so that I can allow God to work in me. I find myself at a constant of pursuing God's light, and it is because of the trials that are before me. Because of my sufferings, I am growing closer to God, breathing deeper, and finding peace in the middle of the storm. I have a new hope that there is going to be an absolute beauty at the end of these trials. Why, you may ask? Because I am working harder and harder to refine myself on this walk with God. If I really want a closer walk with God, I can't keep my dirty life of sin. I am "press[ing] on toward the goal to win the prize for which God has called me heavenward in Christ Jesus" (Phil. 3:14 NIV).

No one likes the process of refining, but the end result is worth the testing, I promise! Momma, what trials are you facing as you mother your children? What impurities are hindering you in those trials that keep you from fully experiencing Christ's inexpressible and glorious joy? I encourage you to pray a bold prayer for God to move on your heart and help you to lay aside your fleshly nature that hinders you from a pure faith in God. The course of action will require many steps, but the process will be worth the time and effort in the end!

DAY 36

Sneaking Food

I knew this day would come. Right after my daughter's diagnosis of type 1 diabetes, the doctor warned me of all the resilient behaviors that would happen, especially during the teenage years. Even the support groups for type 1 parents had me in panic with their posts on Facebook of their child's behavior, seeking help. All the extra worries I knew I would have to face one day crumbled me in fear. Sneaking food, learning to count carbs and dose insulin on her own, anger, depression, questioning God "Why me?" and so much more were all worries that I knew I would have to face one day. The support T1D groups helped tremendously but also had me hiding in fear! With a newly diagnosed T1D, I felt like I had enough worries already and couldn't handle seeing other parents crying for help with new worries I had not faced yet, so I decided to withdraw from the groups momentarily and seek God instead.

God provided help. He provided His peace over the fear. I cried to Him with tears, and He provided encouragement through scripture: "I have told you these things, so that in me you may have peace. In this world you will have trouble. But take heart! I have overcome the world" (John 16:33 NIV).

His peace that transcends all understanding (Phil 4:7)—He gifted to me during the new fears I faced with type 1 diabetes. He even gave me more scripture, reminding me to not worry about tomorrow:

> But seek first his kingdom and his righteousness, and all these things will be given to you as well. Therefore do not worry about tomorrow, for tomorrow will worry about itself. Each day has enough trouble of its own. (Matt. 6:33–34 NIV)

I clang tightly to these verses, taking this new diagnosis one day at a time. Then the day finally came with my daughter sneaking food—a day I had been warned of but I laid aside because God said not to worry about tomorrow. My tomorrow had come, though, and I remembered the Lord's peace that He gave me before and His word to help me through. Honestly, I don't blame my little girl for sneaking food. She *loves* starbursts, and we have to limit her to one or two during mealtime and snack time because of carb counting, insulin dosing, and T1D management. If she did not have diabetes, then she could freely eat all the starbursts she wants, but she cannot. So she has been hiding starbursts and sneaking to eat them when I cannot allow her to have more. Oh, how I wish I could give her more, but T1D does not play fair! Even though the situation is an extra problem, I am also given the opportunity for an extra moment to be God's love.

I embrace my daughter, I let her know why I limit her, and I tell her I know God has big plans for her because of the extra hardship she has to face. We tackle the obstacle together and in God's love. No, she doesn't willingly abide, but I am given an extra moment to teach scripture and help her through her obstacles.

So God gives us His peace yet again that transcends all understanding, and I lay the worry of the day to rest because "tomorrow will worry about itself. Each day has enough trouble of its own." Momma, do you have an extra worry that has not even happened? Do you fear tomorrow even though you do not know what the day will bring? Give that extra problem to God in prayer and ask Him for His peace that transcends all understanding. Let the problem go and take the day one day at a time. Remember, Momma, *you are loved.*

DAY 37

Faithful and True

Before reading today's devotion, take a moment to read Mark 5:25–34. Within these passages, you will find the story of a woman who had a blood issue for twelve years. If you recall, I struggled with this passage in one of my previous devotions, "Even If." Anger blew right through me because I felt like I was forced to encourage my daughter that she could be healed like this woman had been. I did not want to give my daughter false hope because I had false hope. My faith in God was not where it needed to be.

Several months later after enduring multiple broken moments searching for God's heart, this passage was in my morning devotion to read. I reread the story, but this time, I did not become consumed with anger because of the woman's healing. This time, a different concept stood out that I completely missed before.

Jesus was heading to Jairus's home, a man of great wealth and significance, to heal his sick daughter. On the way, the woman who had a blood issue for twelve years desperately sought Jesus and touched His cloak among the multitude who crowded Him. She had such tremendous faith in Jesus that she believed if she could only touch His clothes, she could be made well. Jesus immediately knew power had left Him, so He turned around in the crowd and said, "Who touched My clothes?" (v 30). The disciples thought it was pointless for Jesus to even care who had touched Him because of the great crowd surrounding them. But with this question from Jesus, the new concept from this passage grasped my broken heart—*Jesus sought the woman who sought Him.*

I have read this passage several times and never had this moment opened to my eyes before. The woman had great faith in Christ, faith that I previously did not have! Christ knew someone of great faith was searching for Him, so He sought for His lost sheep among the crowd. Christ did not ignore her in her seeking and even stood still for this unclean, unimportant woman of very low status. Here, Christ proved that status did not matter to Him. What mattered to Him was to save those who were lost and who were in need of just a touch of His clothes. She was so important to Christ that He called her "daughter," and by her faith, she was made well (v 34).

Christ calls us His daughters as well. When we seek Him and are faithful to Him, He is just as faithful back. Isaiah tells us,

> "For the mountains may move
> and the hills disappear,
> but even then my faithful love for your will remain.
> My covenant of blessing will never be broken,"
> says the LORD, who has mercy on you. (Isa. 54:10 NLT)

Though our world may shake and the storm will rage, the Lord's faithful love always remains. When we wholeheartedly seek Him, He seeks us back. Even when we don't seek Christ, He still will give us mercy and love us. He longs for us to come running into His open arms, throwing away our old life of sin to be new in Him. We must never forget that Christ is faithful to His word. We are reminded of Jesus's faithfulness in Second Timothy:

> Here is a trustworthy saying:
> If we died with him,
> we will also live with him;
> if we endure,
> we will also reign with him.

If we disown him,
he will also disown us;
if we are faithless,
he remains faithful,
for he cannot disown himself. (2 Tim. 2:11–13
NIV)

What the Lord says He will do, He will do! He doesn't go back on His word and change His mind. The Bible is a constant, faithful word that never changes. Christ will always be right there with us, enduring the hardships of our storms. But if we disown Him, He will disown us too. Do not fear! Even if we are faithless, He still remains faithful so that we can always have the chance to turn back to His promises. I was of little faith, but He never turned His back on me. Instead, He sought me as I sought Him. Hallelujah! The great victory has already been won by Jesus who is faithful and true (Rev. 19:11). Through the cross and resurrection, He has already defeated all powers of evil.

Life is always changing. If I look back to the beginning of this devotional two years ago, our lives are completely different now. Through all the changes, the Lord has remained faithful and true, letting us know, "Heaven and earth will pass away, but My words will by no means pass away" (Mark 13:31 NKJV).

God is the same today as He has always been. He is our rock, our fortress, and our refuge (Ps. 31:3–4). The Lord is always faithful, even when our days change and we face new challenges. He will always seek us when we seek Him in faith.

DAY 38

Help My Unbelief

I wait for the LORD, my soul waits,
And in His word I do hope.
—Ps. 130:5 NKJV

B efore reading today's devotion, take a moment and read Mark 9:14–29. This passage that we will study today really humbled me when I read the verses. A man with a son who has a mute spirit brought him to Jesus's disciples to be thrown out. The spirit was so corrupt that his son would convulse, foam at the mouth, gnash his teeth, and become rigid. But the disciples could not cast out the bad spirit! Jesus answered the father by saying they were faithless. Jesus meant that with faith in Him, the spirit could have been thrown out.

So they brought the boy to Jesus, and the spirit immediately started to convulse. The devil knew Jesus was stronger and about to cast the spirit out, so he reared his ugliness up. Yet Jesus did not respond immediately to this. Instead, he asks the boy's father, "How long has this been happening to him?" And the father said, "From childhood" (v 21). This statement right here—Jesus could have healed the boy immediately, but He took the time to speak to the boy's father. Jesus took the time to show us that some illnesses need our patience and that the son had the harmful spirit for a while since childhood (just like my daughter with type 1 diabetes).

I am certain that this father, like the woman who had a blood issue for several years and yearned to touch Jesus's coat, yearned for Jesus to heal his son. He longed and prayed fervently for his son's good health! We know this because Jesus cared enough to take the time to ask. Jesus made the effort to search for the woman in the crowd, and He made the effort to display compassion to this father.

The father goes into detail concerning the effects of the mute spirit, how the spirit tried to throw his son both into the fire and into the water to destroy him, which I can relate to my daughter's autoimmune disease. The devil tries so often to harm us with fiery anger and drowning sorrow. The father continues and asks with tears, tears of a long suffering and hurt for his child, "But if You can do anything, have compassion on us and help us" (v 22). This statement right here again—the father had faith in Jesus because he sought help from His disciples, but he didn't have enough belief due to his question "if you can?" Truth be told, Jesus can heal! So Christ responded by saying, "*If you can believe, all things are possible to him who believes*" (v 23). *Full belief.* Not half-hearted belief like I struggle with but full belief that Jesus Christ can do all things—the optimistic, childlike faith that is not bogged down and hindered by the world. Jesus truly called me out with my unbelief, and what the father says next really hit home in my weakness: "Immediately the father of the child cried out and said with tears, 'Lord, I believe; help my unbelief!'" (Mark 9:24 NKJV).

With tears, the hurt of so desperately wanting his son to be healed—earnestly seeking the Lord by claiming, "Help my unbelief!"—moved Jesus to heal the father's son. The disciples asked Jesus why they could not cast out the mute spirit, and Jesus said to them, "This kind can come out by nothing but prayer and fasting" (v 29). For years, this father faced the pain of watching his child battle an illness, and I believe I will have to face a journey where I endure the pain of my daughter's illness. I do not know how long this journey will last, but my belief in Christ's capabilities will be strengthened through prayer and fasting. Saint Augustine wrote, "Faith is to believe what we do not see. The reward of faith is to see what we believe."

"Lord, help my unbelief"—a statement so simple yet so convicting. A new faith created in me to believe that one day my daughter will be healed, even though I cannot see the end result. A new faith created in me to believe that there will be a beautiful reward because I trusted in Jesus's capabilities.

I feel like Thomas, the disciple who doubted that Christ had risen from the dead. He chose to only believe that Christ had risen from the dead if he could see Jesus's nail-marked hands for himself and place his hand into His side. When Christ revealed himself to Thomas, he finally believed! But Jesus told Thomas, "Because you have seen me, you have believed; blessed are those who have not seen and yet have believed" (John 20:29 NIV).

I am brought to tears! Even though I have not seen Christ, even though I have not seen the end result of my daughter's type 1 diabetes, I will be blessed if I believe. I am humbled yet again and grateful for Christ revealing His love to me, a love so deep that I truly cannot comprehend the vastness of the Lord Almighty.

Momma, do you have unbelief like me? Do you have situations that you are facing that hinder your belief in Christ because you cannot see the end result? Cry out to Jesus with all your problems and ask him to help your unbelief. Pray and fast over your situation, strengthening your faith along the way. By the time your fasting is over, the result may not have happened, but your belief in Christ's capabilities will be built up into a stronger foundation and a deeper connection into His love.

DAY 39

A Year of Jubilee

One day, as I was folding the laundry, I remembered that I needed to change my daughter's insulin cartilage because the insulin had expired. I sat down in my favorite dining room chair, the chair that I sleepily sit in almost every morning as I thirst for more of God in His word. I began to change the insulin cartilage from memory, a new routine in our life for almost a year now. I held the almost empty cartilage up to the window, the window I lift my eyes to when I search for God above the mountain line of our home in the valley. I gazed upon the clear liquid that kept my daughter alive, the substance created by man to imitate what my daughter could not produce anymore.

As the expired insulin met the skyline of the heavens, I humble myself, time and time again; and I pondered the story God had written in my heart from a year's worth of pain. I had spent so much time in that exact spot searching for God's goodness, thirsting for His life in the death of my daughter's pancreas. I could see now, as clear as the insulin in my hand, how a year of pain—a year of fear, a year of worry—became a story of a year of hope, a year of peace, a year of a new life granted to me in the bottom of the valley. In the deepest valley of sorrow, I found a new love in God (Ps. 23:4). This was a love, I thought I knew. But He tore apart and resewn it together through grace, forgiveness, and a promise. A promise that, "those who sow with tears will reap with songs of joy. Those who go out weeping, carrying seed to sow, will return with songs of joy, carrying sheaves with them" (Ps. 126:5–6 NIV).

I connected the concept of sowing with the "year of jubilee" passage in Leviticus 25–26 when the Lord spoke to Moses concerning a year of rest after the harvest they had sown. Even though my year of sowing into God's Word isn't the same context that is written in these chapters, I relate to the life from the words as a celebration that will happen for me when I remain faithful through the storm. I have come to find the benefits of a year of jubilee from the sowing of tears that I have poured into His Word and into my children:

> I will put my dwelling place among you, and I will not abhor (reject) you. I will walk among you and be your God, and you will be my people. I am the Lord your God, who brought you out of Egypt so that you would no longer be slaves to the Egyptians; I broke the bars of your yoke and enabled you to walk with heads held high. (Lev. 26:11–13 NIV)

When we sow into the Lord's plan, we will reap His promises. God will live with us while we sow, and nothing will separate His love from us (Rom. 8:35–39). He will walk among us and be our God and our leader, and we will be His people. He will bring us through the suffering so that we will no longer be slaves to the enemy and his lies. He will break the yoke of slavery (v 13 NLT) that holds our heads in shame so that we can walk with our heads held high above the lies, above the pain, with our sight on God's glory. No longer hindered by the sowing that makes us bend over in agony but enabling us to walk upright with God by our side as we sow His word of life into ourselves and into our children. A complete year of God's love poured into our hearts through the storms of life.

And to think, only a year has passed in this diabetic journey, and I now see God's love unraveling before my eyes in ways I have never known. There is so much more to happen in the journey ahead, and I go forward with the excitement, the hope of the return song of joy from the tears I have sown. Galatians 6:9 reminded me, "Let us not become weary in doing good, for at the proper time we will reap a harvest if we do not give up" (NIV).

God has written a new song in my heart—a song of praise in the pain, a song of joy in the trial, a song of renewed faith in the waiting. *I raise a hallelujah* to God in the midst of what the devil intended to destroy (Bethel Music). My God has not forsaken me, and He will not forsake you! I lay aside my old garment of sin and clothe myself in His love, His righteousness.

Thank you, God, for your love in the deepest sorrow of my life. Thank you, God, for a rewritten story of life instead of death. Thank you, God, for allowing me to find your unspeakable joy in the middle of the heartache; a year's worth of tears turned into joy because of the sowing I have made in Your word.

Momma, I share this moment with the hopes that if you are facing a hard year that has drowned you in sorrow, there is hope. I can fully testify of this hope because I have sown into His word with many tears, but I have found the songs of joy in return. Let us weep and sow together so that we may celebrate, not just a year but a life well lived in Christ Jesus, our Lord. Turn your eyes to heaven. God is waiting to rewrite your story.

DAY 40

Coming Full Circle

> For God has not given us a spirit of fear, but of
> power and of love and of a sound mind.
> —2 Tim. 1:7 NKJV

Second Timothy 1:7 is, perhaps, my favorite verse. The verse is the first verse I've practiced learning by heart so that I can repeat the verse in prayer when I am overcome with fear and anxiety. As I've been reading devotions and searching for God, trying to hear Him and crucify my flesh, this verse came into a new light, an old gift of peace renewed and refreshed. The power, the love, and the sound mind God offers are not just empty words used for no reason. These are not words to be repeated with worthlessness but with fullness of God's divine grace.

First, let's start with *power*. I'm not talking about human power but God's power: the power that demolishes strongholds (2 Cor. 10:4 NIV), the power for us who believe in Him, and the power that raised Christ from the grave and seated Him in the place of honor at God's right hand (Eph. 1:19–20). God's power that raised Christ from the dead is the same power He offers us to rid us of our fear. It's a power too grand for my simple mind to understand.

Second is *love*, the love I've been searching for yet haven't had to search for, the love that is already here and has been before I existed. The love I've been allowing myself to live in while walking closer with God is also greater than I'll ever comprehend—a love so marvelous that existed before God made the world.

We were already chosen to be holy in Christ by being adopted through His Son, Jesus Christ. God found great pleasure in desiring to create us, even though He knew we would turn to sin and invite wickedness into our hearts. So much pleasure in our existence that He knew He would have to sacrifice His Son for our sins before He even breathed life into our lungs (Eph. 1:4–6). *Wow!* A love that we only know because God first loved us (1 John 4:19). A love too great for me to fully understand, but I've come to learn to trust in, especially as I speak the verse over my daughter in prayer as she tackles her fears, her Goliath.

Third is a *sound mind.* According to the AMP, NLT, and NIV translations, *sound mind* means "self-discipline [abilities that result in a calm, well-balanced mind and self-control]." A sound mind brings clarity to my mind and silences the fears attacking me. Slowly, step by step, the Lord has been disciplining me, transforming and renewing my mind to exhibit self-control over my fears and anxieties, allowing me to test and approve what God's will is—His good, pleasing, and perfect will (Rom. 12:2). A sound mind gives peace that only Christ can give to us because He became flesh and overcame the world (John 16:33). This was the plan since the beginning, before the world's creation, before our existence, when love was already unfailing for us. This was the love to allow Christ to become flesh and die for our sins so that He could freely give peace to our minds because of His ability to overcome the world. And this was the power to raise Christ from the grave. All His glorious beauty was wrapped up into one perfect gift for us (2 Tim. 1:7). A perfect love and a new gift from my favorite verse was now laid out before my eyes.

All these glorious spirits of God help us defeat the fear from the enemy that comes to steal, to kill, and to destroy (John 10:10). This is the devil's purpose but not our Savior's. Fear is *not* from God! God gives us life and gives it more abundantly: Life through His promises, through His word, through His son dying on the cross and raised from the grave and life that existed before creation, the life breathed into our very lungs when we take our first breath of air. The fear we allowed to enter the world because of sin, God planned before existence to destroy! These beautiful qualities from God (love, power, and sound mind) now live in us (1 John 4:4)!

I started this journey to have a closer walk with God by taking a baby step, learning verses to tackle the enemy with the simplicity of just repeating the verses. Now, my heart is opened to more of His grace and the in-depth power of His word and the power and greatness of God. Oh, how I truly will never fully understand; but I will always long to inch closer and closer, deeper and deeper, falling into His arms as He carries me through. With all this hope and love, I have gained one blessing, one reading, one day at a time. This may be too much grace for my simple mind and human flesh to take in all at once. But God is all knowing and knows what I need when I need it and gives when I am submitting to His will, truly allowing Him to correct me and to discipline me so that I am molded into the person I am to become, slowly maturing my faith through patience in the trial. I have always been loved by God, but I have had to work on myself, to be mature and complete, not lacking anything (James 1:3–4).

With 2 Timothy 1:7, the verse that has helped me tremendously and means so much to me, I am able to offer back to God through my testimony—through me being tested by the fire, through me seeking Him, and through me disciplining myself to come full circle back to Him in a deeper love. I can live in this love daily and into which fall deeper and deeper as I always continue to walk with Him on earth until the day that I am rewarded to walk beside His glorious, radiant beauty in heaven.

Come, I invite you into His grace that has been waiting on you. "You will find that a little talk with Jesus makes it right," we hear from "Just a Little Talk with Jesus" by the Statler Brothers. Jesus will fulfill everything you need, help your situation, and make it right with just a little talk with Him! One prayer at a time, one talk at a time. I praise the Lord now for His love, for forgiveness, for ridding me of my flesh, and for filling me with His Spirit. I will sing now the new song of my journey—"This is my story, this is my song" ("Blessed Assurance"). Church hymns with which I grew up singing are now coming full circle too. The words of worship songs, hymns, and the Bible are not to simply be said and repeated but to fully live in and resonate in your heart. These are words to lift up your soul into God's hands and allow you to walk hand in hand with Him now (James 1:22–25).

Momma, I pray that we will always grow in the Lord and never quit growing. I pray that we will become doers of the word and not just hearers of the word. I pray that my writings have truly helped you know that *you are loved* by me and by the Highest King. All glory and praise go to God for the change He has created in me and I pray that He creates in you too.

> For this reason I kneel before the Father, from whom every family in heaven and on earth derives its name. I pray that out of his glorious riches he may strengthen you with power through his Spirit in your inner being, so that Christ may dwell in your hearts through faith. And I pray that you, being rooted and established in love, may have power, together with all the Lord's holy people, to grasp how wide and long and high and deep is the love of Christ, and to know this love that surpasses knowledge—that you may be filled to the measure of all the fullness of God. (Eph. 3:14–19 NIV)

*****

Thank you, Lord, for the deep drink of your glorious love. I came thirsting for You, and You made my cup overflow. I pray my cup now overflows into each and every momma who reads this devotional, filling them full of your goodness and life. All glory and honor go to you, Lord, for using me to magnify your name so that others will come to live in your love.

AFTERWORD

> And you shall remember that the LORD your God led
> you all the way these forty years in the wilderness, to
> humble you *and* test you, to know what *was* in your
> heart, whether you would keep His commandments
> or not. So He humbled you, allowed you to hunger,
> and fed you with manna which you did not know nor
> did your fathers know, that He might make you know
> that man shall not live by bread alone; but man lives by
> every *word* that proceeds from the mouth of the LORD.
> —Deut. 8:2–3 NKJV

As I reflect on the journey through writing this forty-day devotional, I remember the ways the Lord led me through the wilderness, the unknown situations of type 1 diabetes and parenting,
so that I might be humbled and tested. I truly have been humbled
and tested, but I am so thankful that the enemy did not win and
that I did not give up on searching the Lord's commands to better
myself.

By humbling myself in the testing, I gained stronger faith. God
fed our family with an unknown substance of which neither we nor
our fathers knew nothing that I call type 1 diabetes. God did not
cause the illness, but He could have allowed the autoimmune disease
to happen, like Job's situation in the Bible, and for us to be tested
by the trial. Being tested by the trial did help me understand that we
cannot live by bread alone, the pleasures of life, or by simply reading
the Bible. We *live by every word* that proceeds out of the mouth of the

Lord, allowing Him to be our sustainer. We are reminded of living by God's word in this passage:

> All Scripture is God-breathed and is useful for teaching, rebuking, correcting and training in righteousness, so that the servant of God may be thoroughly equipped [*complete* in NKJV] for every good work. (2 Tim. 3:16–17 NIV)

I experienced a "forty-day journey" in the wilderness, with the Lord correcting me, teaching, rebuking, and training me in righteousness so that I can be complete and wrapped up in God's love and equipped for the days to come. "While it may be necessary to pass through wilderness experiences, one does not have to live there," the description from the book of Numbers in the KJV Bible says. We do not have to live in the wilderness, but we can live on the words of the Lord. Remember, we must "be doers of the word, and not hearers only, deceiving [ourselves]" (James 1:22 NKJV).

I started this journey being a hearer of the word and not a doer of the word. By the trials and testing of fire, I chose to search God's Word more and discovered the life in His word. I will always have this journey to remember how God led me through the wilderness and humbled my heart to His will. The Word prompts us, "The Lord himself goes before you and will be with you; he will never leave you nor forsake you. Do not be afraid, do not be discouraged" (Deut. 31:8 NIV).

The Lord goes before us in all our trials, in every situation we face. Even though we may be tested and make mistakes along the way, He is with us—never leaving, never forsaking. We don't have to fear the unknown and be discouraged by the sight in front of us. In the unknown situations that we face and cannot see the outcome, we can learn to live on the word of God to help sustain us.

Momma, now that you have completed this forty-day journey in love with me, what changes in your heart have you noticed happen? I pray that I have sparked a fire in your heart to reflect on the good, to practice seeking the Lord, and to fully know how deeply loved you are.

ABOUT THE AUTHOR

Kimberly Sexton lives in southern West Virginia where the valleys run low and the mountains climb high. Coal trains breeze by daily past her home, and wildlife add their sweet lullaby underneath the star strung sky. In their home in the valley, you will find Kimberly and her husband working together as they raise their two littles to be wrapped up in God's love.

As an art teacher to elementary students, Kimberly is given the opportunity to let her light shine so that others can be filled with God's grace and mercy. Kimberly also has a passion to encourage mommas to know how truly loved they are as she seeks God to encourage her own heart through the daily tasks of parenting and life. You can find more of her work on her Facebook group called "Momma, You Are Loved."